MW00987451

THE NUMINOUS

TAROT GUIDE

A NEW WAY TO READ THE CARDS

KNOW THE CARDS
TO KNOW YOURSELF

with Rashunda Tramble

aster

First published in Great Britain
in 2021 by Aster, an imprint
of Octopus Publishing Group Ltd,
Carmelite House, 50 Victoria
Embankment, London EC4Y 0DZ
www.octopusbooks.co.uk
www.octopusbooksusa.com

An Hachette UK Company
www.hachette.co.uk

Distributed in the US by Hachette
Book Group, 1290 Avenue of the
Americas, 4th and 5th Floors, New
York, NY 10104

Distributed in Canada by Canadian
Manda Group, 664 Annette St,
Toronto, Ontario, Canada M6S 2C8

ISBN 978-1-78325-442-2

A CIP catalogue record for
this book is available from the
British Library.

Printed and bound in the UK.

10 9 8 7 6 5 4 3 2 1

The 78 plates illustrating the
Major and Minor Arcana are from
designs by Pamela Colman Smith,
reproduced from the unabridged
Dover (2005) republication of the
edition published by William Rider
& Son Limited, London, 1911
under the title *The Pictorial Key
to the Tarot: Being Fragments of
a Secret Tradition under the Veil
of Divination*.

Consultant Publisher: Kate Adams
Art Director: Jaz Bahra
Senior Editor: Leanne Bryan
Copyeditor: Tara O'Sullivan
Designer: Megan van Staden
Production Manager: Caroline
    Alberti

CONTENTS

THE MINOR ARCANA   109

INTRODUCTION

This book is for you.

And you.

And, hey, over there – you too.

The Numinous Guide to Tarot offers a modern, real-life take on the meaning of each card in your deck. But it is also about *you* and how you can use the insights ushered in by the 78 cards that make up the Major and Minor Arcanas to better see yourself and your experiences of daily life.

Yes, the tarot can be of service to the forlorn lover wondering if their paramour will return. But how about the artist trying to land gallery representation? The Magician (see page 25) can show them the way. Meanwhile, a writer might meditate on the Ace of Wands (see page 111) before adding another 1,000 words to their manuscript. And what about the parent who pulls the Six of Pentacles (see page 299) during divorce proceedings, as they ready themselves for a power play?

Or the couple who pulled the Two of Cups (see page 227) last year after their third date, then the Lovers (see page 45) this year and now wonder if it's a positive signal of things to come? And don't forget about the single woman deciding to become pregnant and to parent alone, on her own terms. The Fool (see page 21), so often misunderstood, tells her to trust her intuition and just go for it.

The point is that everything we experience in our daily lives can be viewed through the lens of tarot. And rather than turning to the cards for 'answers', this book is a guide to using your deck to reflect the truths that already live inside you. Tarot has long been thought of as a tool for divination, but it is also about using the hidden codes and messages of the cards as keys to unlock your individual relationship to whatever events are unfolding in your life. It's about using the language of tarot to ask the conscious and unconscious parts of yourself questions and receiving answers that will help both sides of your psyche work together seamlessly. Rather than a tool for 'predicting' future outcomes, the Numinous approach to the tarot is about applying the meaning of the cards to your needs and your life *now*.

WHAT IS THE TAROT?

A tarot deck usually consists of 78 cards and is divided into two parts: the Major Arcana, which has 22 cards; and the Minor Arcana, which has 56. The Major Arcana cards, such as the Fool, the Magician, the High Priestess and so on, introduce the archetypes connected to life overall, its seasons and transitions.

The cards of the Minor Arcana reflect our day-to-day situations, revelations and struggles. These cards are divided into suits, each of which has their own elemental correspondences and properties.

+ **Swords (sometimes called Knives)**: connected to the element of Air. Properties include intelligence, decision-making and logic.

+ **Wands**: connected to the element of Fire. Properties include creativity, action and ideas.

+ **Cups:** connected to the element of Water. Properties include emotions, relationships and desires.

✦ **Pentacles (sometimes called Coins or Discs):** connected to the element of Earth. Properties include security, practicalities and the material world.

Each suit of the Minor Arcana has 14 cards, with each card designated a number or a court name, like a deck of playing cards: Ace, 2–10, Page, Knight, Queen and King.

Don't let the word 'Minor' fool you. This grouping may be connected to the 'small stuff' of our everyday lives, the things we encounter on a daily basis rather than the big, overarching life themes of the Major Arcana, but sometimes something 'minor' can be what sparks a 'major' shift.

A SHORT HISTORY

So where did tarot come from? And how did it become what we know it as today? Depending on whom you believe, tarot is either a gift from the ancient Egyptians and/or Kabbalists, or the descendant of an old Italian card game. Feel free to do your own research, but for the purposes of this book, let's go with the latter.

According to many sources, what's known as 'tarot' today started as a game called '*tarocchi*' in the 15th century. Many decks were created for aristocratic families on special occasions and featured family members as characters in scenes depicted on the cards. As the Church played a major role in society during these times, the images on the cards had predominantly Christian symbolism and themes. Use of tarot as an actual divination tool seemed to start in the 16th century, but it wasn't until around the 1900s that the version of tarot we know today appeared.

The most well-known deck, the Rider-Waite-Smith (RWS), debuted in 1910. It was commissioned by A. E. Waite and realized by the artist Pamela Colman Smith, both members of a secret society called the Golden Dawn. The deck contained the same card numbers, suits and structure as older decks, but some of the card names in the Major Arcana were changed.

For example, the Pope became the Hierophant, and the Papess became the High Priestess, both of the former names reflecting the previous influence of the Church. The deck was published by the William Rider & Son company in the UK, which eventually gave the deck the 'Rider' part of its name.

At this time, tarot cards were relegated to occult groups, alternative shops and 'fortune-teller' booths at amusement parks. It wasn't until the 1970s, when the 'New Age' brought about a resurgence of interest in the esoteric and spiritual worlds, that the practice resurfaced in a more mainstream way.

HOW TO USE THIS BOOK

The RWS deck has spawned many derivatives and systems since its launch in 1910. Now there are esoteric decks, pagan decks, angel decks, LGBTQIA+-centred decks, BIPOC-centred decks and many others. Perhaps you own one – or more – of these. Many of them come with their own guidebook about how to interpret the cards. This is where *The Numinous Guide to Tarot* comes in. This book is written to be your companion with *any* tarot deck, no matter the genre or the style of imagery.

And it isn't just about how to decipher the tarot. Instead, the text for each card connects its meaning to a different life situation, using a story to help you 'embody' the message of the card. The invitation is to put yourself in the shoes of each character you meet along the way. A general meaning of the card follows the story, along with journal prompts you can use to strengthen your relationship to the message of the card and to dig deeply into what it means *for you*. Capture your thoughts about each card and create your own compendium of intimately personal tarot meanings.

The Numinous Guide to Tarot honours the original meanings of the cards, as established decades ago, but it also acknowledges life in the world we inhabit today. This book invites you to connect your story to the examples given to discover the 'whys' behind the events of daily life. Perhaps you'll want to ask a question, then pull a card. Or maybe you'll want to pull a card and *then* ask a question. Or perhaps you don't have a specific question to ask. If that's the case, don't worry; just pull a card and see what comes up.

It's up to you.

This book is written for any reader of the tarot, at any level of experience or skill. Whether you're a complete newbie who's just starting your tarot journey, or an expert with decades of experience, this book contains insights, inspiration and perhaps some surprising plot twists that will help you further your understanding of tarot, yourself and your life.

Feel free to doodle in this book, to dog-ear its pages and do whatever you like to make it yours. We wrote it for you and it's about each and every aspect of the humanity that makes you the unique individual that you are.

HOW TO PULL A CARD

You may be expecting to read that the best way to pull a tarot card is to grab your deck, lock yourself in a room, sit cross-legged in the middle of a circle of crystals, light a candle, close your eyes and then pull a card.

This is valid and beautiful. But it's just one way.

Pulling a tarot card can be as spiritual or mundane as you'd like it to be. You might choose to use the method above; you might feel comfortable just pulling a card during your morning commute. Whatever your approach, the most important thing to remember is to ground, connect with your deck and then pull.

Here's an example of how to do this:

If possible, make sure both your feet are flat on the ground or floor. If this isn't possible, try to make physical contact with something that is touching the ground. Hold your deck face-down in one hand and place your other hand on top. Close your eyes. Breathe softly and easily. Then, sense your feet connecting to the ground (or the object that is touching the ground). Imagine a ball of energy slowly building under you. Allow the ball of energy to gently float up your body and imagine it enveloping your hands, then travelling up the rest of your body and out of the top of your head. Imagine it rising to the ceiling (or sky), then slowing down and making a return trip through your body and back to the ground.

Now open your eyes and shuffle the cards for about ten seconds. Pull one card from the top of the deck and turn it over.

THE
MAJOR
ARCANA

O

THE FOOL .

THE FOOL

Imagine coming home after a 12-hour day in the office. As you walk through the living room, you pass your housemates lounging on the sofa. They look up at you longingly and ask, 'What's for dinner?'

You always either cook dinner or pick up a takeaway on the way home for everyone at the flat. You're the most responsible of them all. But tonight is different. You were swamped all day and missed lunch, which meant you hadn't eaten since that morning, so you treated yourself to an early dinner at that new Vietnamese place around the corner before heading home.

'I have no clue,' you answer, as you rub your full belly. 'But good luck finding out.'

It's freeing not to have all the answers – or dinner – for everyone.

We begin our trip through the Major Arcana with the Fool, assigned the number zero, signalling a new start. Nothingness. Get your deck, find the card and pull it out. Look at it. Really look at it. What do you see? Most decks show a figure standing almost on the edge of a cliff. One more step and then… Will they fall? Will they fly? Do they even care? Perhaps those fluttering sleeves will turn into wings.

In historical decks, the Fool was the court jester or the village idiot. In modern decks, the Fool can prompt you to follow your heart and accept the risks involved. Depending on the situation, the Fool can also warn you about shirking responsibilities or leaping before looking.

The Fool can also help you to start a new phase in life or take on a new challenge, guided only by your intuition and faith. The Fool is you as a child: when you knew how to fly; when you could be anything and everything you wanted; when society's expectations of you, low or high, had no impact; when you refused to be weighed down by other people's opinions of what the correct path for you should be. There's a whole world out there waiting for you to explore. All you have to do is have faith, take a leap and begin.

JOURNAL PROMPTS

+ Think of a time in your life when you felt under pressure to know everything and to carry it all, no matter how tired or burned out you were, no matter how sick you were, no matter how overwhelmed you were. How much of that pressure came from external sources? How much of it came from you? Free-write on how things would have played out differently if you'd freed yourself of the responsibility to please others and get it all right and acted purely on instinct instead.

+ Think of a person whom you admire for the way they always take the initiative and act on their dreams. Perhaps it's somebody famous, or maybe it's somebody in your life. List all the qualities they embody. Which of these could you apply to the situation you are currently facing?

+ What fears are holding you back? Think of an area where you are being asked to stretch beyond your comfort zone and where it's also impossible to know how things will play out. Write about the worst-case scenario if things were to go wrong. Where do these fears come from? What would you do if they were to come true?

THE MAGICIAN.

THE MAGICIAN

You have a film inside you that's waiting to be made, but you keep putting it off. It centres around a Great Big Love Story™ you've had in your head for years. It's been gestating and wants to spring forth.

And you really want to make it happen.

But first, you need to take another course in that editing software you've been planning to get to grips with. You actually took a course on the same programme last year, but the course being offered now is an updated version. You need to read another book for research, learn that new graphics programme or speak to a few more relationships experts.

Or perhaps you just need to actually start writing the screenplay. Yes, it's always great to learn new things, but it's even better to use the skills you already have. Be sure of yourself and what you already know and get moving.

The Magician is card number one. Find the card in your deck and take it out. The Magician is usually depicted as someone standing behind a table loaded with the tools of their trade, which mirror the suits of the tarot deck: a wand, a cup, a pentacle and a sword. The Magician knows how to use each of these tools with dexterity.

The Magician represents focus, skill, ability, action and, yes, magic. They've studied and practised. Now they are ready to perform. When the Magician appears, the card is asking you to believe that you can do anything you set your mind to. It's asking you to reach down deep into your lived experiences and retrieve your confidence.

It's normal to question your own ability when faced with a big project or task. And when that project or task is close to your heart, self-doubt magnifies.

'Am I the right person to do this? Do I have what it takes to make this idea become a reality?'

The Magician says: 'Yes, you are. And yes, you do.'

You have the gifts. You have everything you need.

The Magician's tools, which, like the tarot suits, reflect the elements of creation (Fire, Water, Earth and Air) are laid out on the table and ready for you to use. You don't need another course or another book. You don't need another app. You have the skills. You have the knowledge. You have a direct link to the source of all creation. The Magician says: 'Stop procrastinating and just do it.'

JOURNAL PROMPTS

+ List all the things you know you're good at. These could be innate talents that you've always had a flair for, or subjects and skills that you've mastered with study and effort. If you get stuck, include the things you get complimented on and that others always seem to notice about you. Which of these skills or abilities could be applied to your current situation?

+ Set aside some time to meditate and, before you begin, set an intention to receive divine guidance and insight that can be applied to birthing your next big project. If you're not currently working on anything, you can also ask to be shown what your next project might be. Write down your intention and read it to yourself before you set your timer. After you have completed your meditation, note down anything that came through for you.

+ How does your fear of being seen manifest? Are you worried about messing up? Being ridiculed? Inadvertently hurting others by speaking up? Notice if any of these fears are present in your current situation and whether they may be preventing you from going all in with your creative process.

THE HIGH PRIESTESS

THE HIGH PRIESTESS

You're mysterious and grandmotherly. The kids in the neighbourhood call you 'the Oracle' after the character in *The Matrix* movie series. She was the mysterious soul who served as a counsellor of sorts to Neo (also known as 'the One', played by Keanu Reeves) and gave him guidance on how to battle the Matrix.

Just like the Oracle, you enjoy baking, smoking cigarettes and dishing out prophecy. You're a combination of opposites, embodying a duality: while motherly and caring, you also enjoy making people uncomfortable, especially the young folks who pass by and pay their respects as you hold court on your front porch. For example, you question their choice of music as it booms from their cars. You ask if they really know the meanings of the lyrics. But you do it not to be a grump, but for the sake of helping them grow. To become aware. Your job is to unbalance the Matrix in order to break a cycle.

In the tarot, the Oracle and the High Priestess have a lot in common. The third card of the Major Arcana, carrying the number two, the High Priestess is known as the 'spiritual mother figure' of the major grouping. Most decks show the High Priestess sitting on a throne between two columns, facing us, wearing a crown of moon phases, with a crescent resting at her feet. When this card appears, the High Priestess is asking you to break out of the comfort of what you perceive as 'reality' – your own version of the Matrix – and instead to lean in to your intuition. She wants you to believe in the power of your unconscious and to honour the hairs that stand up on the back of your neck. She also wants you to look deeper into the meanings of situations; to go beyond the veil and figure out *why*.

Be brave enough to step behind the curtain and walk out toward the sea.

The High Priestess can guide you in finding an alternative path that will help you unlock your secrets. She does this by urging you to reach deep inside to rediscover your psychic powers and connect with your spirit guides. She reminds you to start living and working your magic in alignment with the phases of the moon.

This card can also signal that now is a time for privacy, for making some space so you can touch base with your inner world. Her columns represent the doorway to your own personal sanctuary, the place where you go to connect to your subconscious, to block out the external world and allow your intuition to bubble up. What truths do you think you will discover when you retreat into this space?

JOURNAL PROMPTS

+ What part of your 'reality' are you currently questioning? Free-write about a situation or scenario that doesn't quite 'add up' for you. Perhaps it's a relationship where you find yourself questioning the other person's motives, or a work situation where you suspect there's more going on behind the scenes than meets the eye. What could you do to get more clarity?

+ Think about a time when your intuition spoke to you. What was the quality of this 'voice'? How did you hear it? What did it say to you? Now give your intuitive voice a name, to distinguish it from the voice of your ego/thinking mind. Practise dialoguing with it in the coming days, either in your head or in your journal.

+ Where can you go to be alone? Where can you go to find solitude? Is it your bedroom? Your shower? Taking a drive to nowhere by yourself? Wherever it is, this card is asking you to make time in the coming days to be by yourself and with yourself in stillness.

THE EMPRESS.

THE EMPRESS

You've been sitting in front of your piano for what seems like hours. Actually, it has been hours. Which have turned into days. And you're at a loss. You've been given the chance to score your first film. It's a short one, but it's by the hottest fashion designer of the moment and they're making their first foray into film. You're not even sure how it happened: the designer happened upon your Mixcloud account and listened to one of your tracks. Then another. Then another.

A few messages and conference calls later, you're on your way to becoming an 'official' composer. Or, at least, you would be if you could just, well, compose. But all you can do right now is cry. The pressure to create on someone else's schedule and budget is just too much. But create you must.

This is your chance to make a mark on, if not the world, then at least the industry. Because of how hard you worked and the way you scraped and saved and made sure you were prepared for the moment when you got the chance to manifest your dream, you've shown that you're not just a musician, you're a creator. And your child is ready to be born.

The Empress is card number three in the Major Arcana and depicts the archetype of both the mother and the goddess. Similar to the High Priestess, she is warm and caring. But whereas the High Priestess invites you to connect to your inner power, the Empress encourages you to use your power in the external world. This power can manifest itself in many ways.

The Empress is depicted sitting on a throne surrounded by wheat, trees and a flowing creek. This card can be extremely complicated for some. On one hand, the Empress is the epitome of 'womanhood' and, in some decks, this means pregnancy. To those who identify as women and haven't had children, either by choice or by chance, this association can feel clunky and limiting.

But when this card appears, remember that a 'child' can take various forms – as can the energy of nurturing. A child can be a melody in your head yearning to become a song. It can be your plan to run for city council. It can be that vegan taco business you've always wanted to start. The Empress is reminding you to give your child what it needs to thrive in the world: food, water and nutrients, and also encouragement, patience, love, etc. And if *you* are that child, then, yes, you need the same.

The Empress also asks us to unravel words such as 'fertility' and 'birthing' and to experience the power of linking these words to our thoughts and dreams. But check your attachment to your ideas. Once you birth them and send them out into the world, that's it. You have to let them go and be free.

JOURNAL PROMPTS

- List all of the attributes you associate with 'maternal love'. This may or may not be a reflection of the mothering you received yourself and that's okay. In what ways do the different people in your life exhibit these qualities? How do you embody them yourself? How could you 'mother' the situation you are facing?

- What are you currently 'birthing'? This may not be obvious at first, so take your time to consider where fresh green shoots are appearing in your life. What do you need to 'feed' them in order to give them space to grow and mature? What action can you take today to fertilize their soil?

- Write a letter as if to your own mother, letting her know what you appreciate about the way she mothered you and what you wish you had been able to receive from her. This letter is not something you ever need to share with her unless you feel called to do so. Take your time and try to write from a 'neutral' place, simply observing your experience of mothering without placing blame for anything she may have got 'wrong'. What are you grateful for about the way you were mothered? What would you do differently? What do you wish your mother had known about how to give you what you need and how can you give this to yourself now?

THE EMPEROR.

THE EMPEROR

Your phone buzzes. It's *that* friend. The one who calls you whenever they need something, which is at least once a week. Sometimes they just want to vent and know you will happily lend your ear. Well, maybe not happily, but you listen anyway, because you don't want to hurt their feelings. Setting boundaries has never been your strong point when it comes to your friend. Actually, setting boundaries has never been a strong point in many aspects of your life.

But today is different. You're working late because you have a deadline. You're tired. You want to go home. Being a sponge for somebody else's stuff is exactly what you don't need right now. The phone continues to buzz and finally you answer. But instead of your normal reply, you stop, take a breath and say: 'Actually…'

The Emperor represents power, rules and authority – the father figure archetype. The Emperor is often shown sitting on a stone throne with mountains behind him, a reflection of the stability and stoicism that inform his actions.

The meaning of the Emperor has evolved over time. The symbolism noted above says it all: the Emperor has traditionally been read as firm and dependable, almost rigid. He lays down the law and will not budge. Through a more fluid lens, this limited depiction of a 'patriarchal' masculine becomes associated with punishment and an oppressive approach to 'law and order'.

Meanwhile, we forget that this energy can also protect us when enacted for the greater good. This is the other side of the Emperor, where he represents safety, security and fighting for what's right. The Emperor can ensure the rights of the people in his empire are protected. As much as he can be bossy, he can be benevolent as well.

When this card shows up, it's asking you to consider where you could set better boundaries, lay down some limits and rewrite your own rule book, the better to serve and protect yourself first and foremost. The Emperor is card number four, which can represent containment: the metaphorical 'four walls' you use to protect your domain, as well as the borders and criteria for who can cross them.

The Emperor can also hint that it's time to take greater responsibility for your actions – and for any fear-based inaction.

It takes courage to own your part in life not going your way, especially if this means going against 'the rules' of how things should be done.

Meditate on the Emperor when you need to steady your spine and stand up to the status quo. If you're uneasy with confrontation, imagine becoming so still, stoic and sure of yourself, seated on the Emperor's throne, that you are able to handle whatever sticks and stones may be thrown at you. Write your own rules and be confident in standing up for what's right for you.

JOURNAL PROMPTS

+ When was the last time you called somebody out for wrongdoing? Write about this situation and explore the energy of righteousness that gave you the courage to take a stand. What was it about the situation that helped you override any fear of conflict and do 'the right thing'? How is this being reflected in your current circumstances?

+ Bring to mind an important decision you have to make. Which way would you go if your only concern was to protect your own interests? Use the Emperor's courage to put a boundary around your time and energy and take aligned action that's in service of your material and emotional sovereignty.

THE HIEROPHANT

THE HIEROPHANT

Your grandmother was interesting. Armed with a sharp wardrobe and a tongue to match, M'dear (short for 'Mother Dear') was the most beautiful thing to ever come out of Coahoma County, Mississippi, and was almost never seen in public without her red lipstick. It didn't matter if she was going to the grocery store, the gas station or down the driveway to the mailbox, M'dear always made sure her make-up was on point.

She handed this tradition down to your mother and sister, but you couldn't be bothered with the hassle of it all – until you turned 48.

Perhaps it was because your mother had just passed, or perhaps you were just homesick, but for some reason, you started wearing red lipstick. And not just for nights out on the town; you'd sometimes apply your lippy just to go shopping.

Of all the traditions from your family and culture, M'dear's red lipstick is the one that you treasure the most.

Passing on a tradition is one of the meanings associated with the Hierophant, card number five in the Major Arcana. This is reflected in the scene usually shown on the card: the Hierophant sits on a raised throne as they instruct two figures at their feet.

As with the Empress and Emperor, the classic reading of Hierophant energy can feel dated today: orthodoxy, secret rites and tradition. When used to wield power over others, these attributes can be a curse. But when taught under the auspices of the modern Hierophant, ancient customs, practices and rituals can also be read as blessings and a way of transferring divine knowledge to prepare the generations to come to go out into the world.

The Hierophant wants you to contemplate what you have inherited, the traditions you hold on to, the patterns you've carried over from your younger years – and why. How do you know what you know, or, rather, what you *think* you know? What parts of your ancestry or culture do you relate to and hold dear and how are you honouring these parts of your lineage?

This card also asks you to take a look at your gurus: have you placed them on a pedestal? If so, why? What are you getting out of their words and teachings? There's nothing wrong with admiring a learned person, but leave room for yourself on that perch.

JOURNAL PROMPTS

+ What are you learning and what are you qualified to teach? Reflect on a recent experience where you felt you learned something about yourself and the world. If you were going to turn this into a course, or write a book on the subject, what would the title be? What key lessons would you want to pass on to your students or readers?

+ List several of the 'life lessons' your early caregivers (parents, grandparents, teachers, etc.) taught you by example. How did the way they embodied these principles in their lives influence you and how could adhering to any attendant beliefs about 'how the world is' be helping or hindering you with your current situation? For each thing you write down, consider a person or teaching that models a different way of doing things. What can you learn from them?

+ Think about somebody you consider to be particularly 'wise' or 'enlightened'. Where do you think they got their knowledge from? Write an imaginary application for an internship with them and tell them all the things you'd like to learn from them. When you're finished, consider how you could begin your own journey of discovery, with or without their help.

THE LOVERS.

THE LOVERS

'You can't expect anybody else to love you if you don't love yourself'. You've heard this line a thousand times from your best friend. They mean well, but each time they say it, it stings. You get the gist of it, you really do. But love isn't that simple.

Social media, television, magazines, marketers and society overall have fed you a constant diet of self-doubt. You actually believe that you're not thin enough, your teeth aren't straight enough, your skin isn't light enough, your hair isn't smooth and silky enough… that nothing about you is *enough*. But there's a way to stop the madness. Before you can learn how to love yourself, you first need to unlearn your habit of hating yourself. And you're ready for the universe to teach you that lesson.

You imagine travelling back in time to when the message that you were inherently unlovable began to take hold. You locate that version of yourself, grab them by the arm, pull them through the years and show them who you are and where you are today. Your two selves meet, talk and walk each other through the societal messaging towards a destination: self-love. This is the process of unlearning.

This brings us to card number six, the Lovers. This card is associated with duality and represents, well, yes, love, but not quite romantic love as we know it. The Lovers card can signal love for yourself or an aspect of yourself; love for your family; love for a culture. The Lovers card symbolizes a love that makes you whole.

The card usually depicts two people facing each other as a winged figure hovers above. The Lovers card asks: are you 'whole' within yourself? Meaning, are you accepting of yourself and all of your wonderful parts?

Are you in conference with both your bright shiny lights and the beautiful dark shadows of your soul? Cultivating an understanding and a level of shame-free acceptance for all that we may perceive as both 'good' and 'bad' about ourselves is the key to true self-love.

Of course, the Lovers card can reflect the energy of partnership and even marriage. But rather than this being the 'goal,' it signals that you are open to inviting new relationships and also available for the work of strengthening your current bonds with others.

The perfect love doesn't exist, but the Lovers card asks you to enjoy the journey as we discover what true love – what *union* – means to us.

JOURNAL PROMPTS

+ Write a letter to your younger self, at the age when you first came upon the idea that any part of you was 'not okay'. Acknowledge why your younger self came to feel that way and draw their attention to all the different factors at play. What can you say to help them think differently about themselves? Tell them whatever they need to hear in order to heal and remember exactly how loveable they are.

+ What are your love patterns? Note down the role you tend to assume in a partnership and all the ways in which this plays out. For each thing you write down, note what you 'get' out of behaving this way and how this makes you feel. This may bring up 'positive' and 'negative' feelings. Which patterns are you ready to strengthen and which are you evolving beyond?

+ What situation in your life is trying to 'make love' to you? Perhaps it's an idea you're being seduced by, a project you want to give more of yourself to, or a person you can't stop thinking about (romantically or otherwise). What part of you is being called forth into relationship with this person or thing? What would help you feel more worthy of having them or it be part of your life?

THE CHARIOT.

THE CHARIOT

'Tell me: why should we hire you?'

When this question is posed during a job interview, it's usually the cue for you to recite your laundry list of qualifications and accomplishments. You've memorized every detail, so you're ready.

You eagerly run through your education and work experience. You make sure to mention that you're a team player and that you're willing to give it your all to make sure your prospective line manager has the support she needs for the department to be successful. You slide in little bits about the hobbies you think make you seem like a well-rounded and cool person.

You say all the right things. So you wonder why you don't get a second interview?

Perhaps it's because the next person who is interviewed has exactly the same qualifications, but they are able to demonstrate one quality you perhaps lacked: stamina.

It's one thing to be good at what you do and another to be able to do whatever it takes to reach your goals.

If you need the inspiration to make this happen, the Chariot is here to help. Card number seven of the Major Arcana normally depicts a person in a cart or carriage being pulled by two animals.

The Chariot helps us reflect on our desires and what motivates us towards attaining them. It pushes us forwards and gives us the confidence to not only set off in pursuit of our dreams, but to believe in our ability to grasp them, no matter what. Being successful in reaching our goals may very well involve leaving our comfort zones in the dust, just as the chariot rider has left the confines of their village far behind.

Meditate on the Chariot card when you need fuel for your desires and when you need to stay on track and avoid distractions as you work towards your goal. Adopt the rider's straight, steady stance when walking into a tough meeting where you're determined to get the results you want, or stepping into a restaurant with a soon-to-be-ex partner.

This card also gives you permission to believe in yourself and to fluff your own ego a tad, although not to the point of arrogance. The Chariot helps you to give yourself the kind of pep talk that will get you over the finish line when the going gets tough. You're stronger than you feel and wiser than you know: you got this.

JOURNAL PROMPTS

+ Bring to mind a current goal or objective and do an old-school SWOT (strengths, weaknesses, opportunities and threats) analysis of the situation. What hidden strengths can you draw on and what weaknesses do you need to compensate for? What opportunities can you capitalize on and what potential threats lie ahead? With all this down on paper, make a plan of action and commit to it.

+ Think back to a time when you overcame a challenge, against all odds. Was it something physical? Or the emotional challenge of going outside your comfort zone? List all the inner qualities you were able to draw on in this situation. How could you apply some of these to the circumstances you are currently facing?

+ Name something you want that you are unsure you will ever get. List everything that is driving this desire. What makes you want it so much? Now list all the reasons you think you can't or won't get it. Where do these blocks come from? Review both lists and journal about whatever comes up for you.

STRENGTH

You've just posted a social media update and it's getting tons of likes. 'Coming off a 12-hour shift and I'm now off to work on my master's thesis! Yes! #imeverywoman #girlboss #sleepisforsuckas.' Your followers reply with fervour: 'YAAAS QUEEN!' 'YOU GO GIRL!' 'YOU GOT THIS!' No question, you've got it going on. Your accounts show you working, studying, taking care of your children, receiving awards – hell, even skydiving. They display the amazingly productive, smiling, positive person you present yourself to be.

What they don't show – and what people don't see – is that you're tired. And not just tired as in you need a quick nap. Tired as in, 'My feet are dragging. I can't make it up the stairs. And I'm close to burning out.' But you can't break. You have to keep going. If you actually open up and let not just your online followers, but your close friends and family know just how exhausted you are, they might realize that you're a real-life vulnerable soul who needs a time-out. Acknowledging that you're not a superhero to those around you – and yourself – requires vulnerability. And strength.

The Strength card is number eight in the Major Arcana. The card shows a person gently opening a lion's mouth. An infinity symbol hovers over their head. The card traditionally represents overcoming adversity, grace under pressure and using 'soft power' to smooth out a rough situation. The person on the card is usually what people notice first and their bravery and ability to stroke the lion into compliance is applauded.

But which figure on the card do you identify with most – the person or the lion? There's a strong chance it's the former, but let's make a switch. Just for today, identify with the lion – a reflection of power, sovereignty and courage. Yes, this is you.

Meditate on the Strength card to find the strength to let go, to be vulnerable. Allow the person to open your mouth. If you wanted to, you could injure them with just one move. But you don't, because you're strong. When you're strong enough to soften, to say you need help or admit that you're tired, you're taking charge. You're letting someone or something else take the worry and do the work for you. What if the person on the card is actually helping you to relax? Perhaps that open mouth is even a yawn.

The Strength card asks you to be strong enough to say you need help, because you know your worth and will do what it takes to protect your fierce power. It asks you to say 'no' when you don't feel like going out because you know it will sap your energy. It pleads with you to let go of suspicion and allow someone else to help you, not because they want something in return, but because they love you. We can't be strong all the time. And it takes strength to say that.

JOURNAL PROMPTS

+ Are you 'muscling through' a challenging situation for the sake of saving face? Write down everything that comes up when you think about what fears lie beneath your unwillingness to admit you need help, or that you're close to burnout. Are you worried that somebody else will steal your thunder? That the job won't get done properly? Get clear on what exactly you're afraid of.

+ What could you give yourself today to support your inner strength? Consider what part of you feels like it could use a hand and what tools, practices and self-care props you can use to give yourself a boost. Perhaps you need to schedule in time for a nap, or perhaps there's somebody you can call to help you tackle your to-do list. Reach for whatever it is without shame.

+ Write about something you've been putting off because it scares the hell out of you. Is it a difficult conversation? Rising up to meet a challenging deadline? Putting yourself out there on social media? Note down all the details and write about why you find this situation so frightening. Now picture yourself after doing whatever it is. How do you feel?

IX

THE HERMIT.

THE HERMIT

You're a loner. Being a loner has its good and bad points, as you've learned throughout your life. One big plus is that you have more than enough time and space to be with your thoughts, to process your emotions and centre yourself. One big minus, though, is... that you have more than enough time and space to be with your thoughts, to process your emotions and centre yourself. That repetition is intentional. What makes being a loner so alluring to some is the same as what makes it slightly confusing to others.

'There she goes again, going off to lunch by herself,' your co-workers say. 'Strange.'

'Oh my gosh, you meditate every morning? Why?' your roommate asks.

The life of the loner may seem like a masterclass in navel gazing to some, but solitude and contemplation have been useful tools for seekers like yourself since the beginning of time. They honour the art of self-discovery. And that's what you are doing: searching. But you're also drawing people to you with your search.

Card number nine of the Major Arcana is the Hermit. They are alone, but not lonely. Their mind is occupied with their quest for self and the quest to draw like minds to them. The card usually shows a hooded figure standing alone on a peak. They're holding a lamp that seems to light their way in the darkness. If the Hermit calls to you, it's a sign for you to seek solitude and to do so without guilt or feeling the need to explain why. The card asks you to trust the path you're on and have faith that it will lead you where you need to go.

Remain silent. Keep your plans to yourself. Work alone.

The Hermit can also signal that, if you have to make a choice between going along with the group or setting out alone, moving forwards solo may be the best option. You know what's best for you. Follow your own lantern's flame, for your flame serves a dual purpose here: it illuminates your path and it also shines a light for others to follow you. The same people who question your reasons for breaking off from the pack probably want to do the same; they just don't know how. The Hermit prepares you to lead, even if that's not your goal. As you discover more about your inner self, you will lead others to an exploration of this part of themselves. Is this a big responsibility? Yes. But that's part of your journey.

There's a reason why this card speaks to you. It prepares you to find yourself, so that others can find you.

JOURNAL PROMPTS

+ How do you feel about 'alone time'? Do you welcome it and make space for it in your calendar, or do you secretly do anything you can to avoid being alone with your thoughts? If it's the former, get even more intentional with it this week, putting aside some specific time to settle deeply into communion with yourself. If it's the latter, do some gentle self-enquiry around what you fear about being alone.

+ Write about your dream solo 'retreat'. Where in the world would you go and what sort of environment would you choose for your period of self-imposed exile? When you're clear on all the details, you can use this visual as an aid to help you in your meditation and to promote a sense of inner peace and stillness the next time you sit.

+ What do you most long to 'know' about yourself? Write a list of questions to ask yourself that will help you get to the bottom of this. Put aside some time to answer them, one by one, as honestly as you can. Journal about what you uncover.

WHEEL of FORTUNE.

THE WHEEL OF FORTUNE

It's your big day. You've finally snagged an audition to become a member of the city's gospel choir. There aren't too many spots, but you sent your demo reel in anyway. Again. When the invitation to appear in front of the panel arrived in your inbox, you couldn't believe it.

So you've been practising 'His Eye is on the Sparrow' (Whitney's version) over and over. And last night, you double-checked the bus and train routes, just to be sure of arriving on time. The audition schedule is tight: each hopeful has only five minutes to impress the panel.

Your plan to arrive with 30 minutes to spare was watertight. Or it would have been, if only your bus hadn't got stuck in traffic. Which made you miss the non-stop train. Which has made you 15 minutes late to the audition. They're sorry, they tell you, but they just can't fit you in.

What do you learn from this? Shit happens. You can either crawl back home and feel sorry for yourself, or you can stop at a stationery shop on the way and buy a card for each member of the panel, to thank them for at least considering you.

And that's what the Wheel of Fortune is about. Card number ten normally has a wheel in the middle, with mystical beings lining the rim. In the four corners of the card we see even more mystical beings. So many images. So many meanings. So many combinations. Just like life! The Wheel of Fortune reminds us of this. But it also reminds us that 'going with the flow' may be the best way to address a situation. Those mystical animals lining the wheel's rim? They're holding on as it turns, using all their strength, even in the face of centrifugal force, to hang on.

What happens when you zoom out and look at a difficult situation from all aspects? What can be learned? What can be changed? Do you have the patience to wait until things turn in your favour? The Wheel also advises you to be open to chance and the unexpected. To buckle up and go along for the ride. You can't control each and every aspect of your life, but you can control how you respond to the different situations that arise.

JOURNAL PROMPTS

+ How would seeing your current situation from a different angle help you change how you respond to it? Write down anything you perceive as challenging or unfair about what has transpired. Now, choose to view the situation and your response to it from a completely neutral point of view. From this perspective, what is it teaching you about yourself? How might this inform the next action you take?

+ Think about a time when things didn't go as planned and you gained valuable life experience as a result. Perhaps it was being made redundant from a job, which led to you pursuing a new course of study. Maybe a trip got cancelled and instead you discovered a new place to visit close to home. Now bring to mind your current situation and list all the alternative outcomes should things go 'wrong'.

+ Make a mini altar to give thanks to where you're at right now on your journey through life. Gather together any talismans, trinkets and totems that remind you of how you got where you are today and arrange them on your bookshelf, windowsill or desk. Let them remind you that you can never be in control of all the disparate factors at play in any situation.

JUSTICE

You really need them to pay you back, but you're too nice to ask. Your dear friend always has money issues and, yet again, they couldn't pay their bills. So they came to you for a loan. That was six months ago.

You've just checked your own bank account and things are going to be tight this month: rent, your student loan payment, helping out the folks. Having your friend repay their loan would help you to break even. But standing up for yourself has never been your strong point.

You always get the bill at lunch, or go halves when they're the ones ordering steak and you're the vegetarian. You loan them your best outfits and your clothes come back dirty, torn or both, with neither an apology nor an offer to repair them.

You love your friend and the last thing you want to do is endanger your relationship. But how can you endanger a relationship that's already this unbalanced?

The situation with the loan isn't about hurt feelings. It's about money. Your money. And the 'right thing' to do in this situation is to ask for it back.

The Justice card is number 11 in the Major Arcana. It usually shows a person sitting on a throne and wearing a crown, with a sword in one hand and scales in the other. Justice weighs each situation, looking at the pros and cons, what's 'right' and what's 'wrong'. They believe in making things right; their mantra is, 'What's fair is fair'. This is their court. And their decisions are final.

Use the Justice card as inspiration when you need to take a few steps back and look at the cold, hard facts; when things have got emotionally heated and out of balance and you need a clean perspective to get back on track.

Justice also asks us to weigh what you're putting into a situation against what you're getting out of it. Are you getting what you deserve? Are you standing up for yourself and your needs? Is the energy you are putting into a relationship equal to what is being offered back to you?

And don't forget the literal meaning of 'justice' and how it applies to us as global citizens. The Justice card asks us to speak up when we see our fellow community members being subjected to injustice. It asks us to put tender feelings aside and fight for what we know is right.

JOURNAL PROMPTS

+ What feels 'unjust' about your current situation? Write down whatever comes up when you consider this, then go through your list and notice anything that's more about hurt feelings or things being 'unfair' than it is about the facts. If this situation were being judged in a court of law, what would the jury decide? What would need to happen to make things right?

+ List all the injustices you can perceive in the world. Perhaps it's police brutality, or the destruction of the Amazon rainforest. For each one, note down the motivating factors behind these acts: fear, greed, ignorance? Now consider where in your own life you might be perpetuating an injustice for one of the same reasons. What can you do to begin to make it right?

+ Create a character for your inner Justice. What do they look like? What are they wearing and how do they talk? Spend some time in dialogue with this part of yourself and let them know you will be calling on them anytime you need a clear eye on an emotionally complex situation.

XII

THE HANGED MAN.

THE HANGED MAN

That temper tantrum was epic. Absolutely epic. First your beloved child screamed at you, then came the tears. And finally, she threw her backpack on the floor and stormed off to her room.

You'd think she would have changed her tactics by the age of 21.

The former version of you would have risen to the occasion by screaming, crying and stamping in reaction to your daughter's behaviour. Perhaps you would have also tossed in a couple of choice swear words as you told her she was turning out just like your ex. Perhaps you would have ordered her to come out of her room, knowing that she wouldn't.

But you know better these days. You know to stop, count to 10 and wait until she calms down. In the face of a meltdown, the new you does nothing – which is something. This is Hanged Man energy in action.

The Hanged Man represents letting go of the need to control, which actually helps us retain control of ourselves. The keyword for this card is 'surrender'. Number 12 in the Major Arcana, the card shows a person hanging upside down from a tree by one foot, with this leg stretched out. The other leg is bent at the knee. They are not in distress. In fact, they could be meditating.

The Hanged Man is looking at their surroundings from a different viewpoint: upside down. As a result, they see a different way of going about things. They're also forced to be still and to wait. Instead of prodding at a situation or escalating things further, they remain quiet and merely observe. For the Hanged Man, patience isn't just a virtue. It is a necessity.

There's also a sense of martyrdom with this card. The Hanged Man is giving up their normal way of thinking and behaving for the greater good. When you pull the Hanged Man, focus more on what you're *not* doing rather than thinking about what move you could make next. The Hanged Man is asking you to pause before you act. To allow time for contemplation and reflection. They are drawing your attention to the fact that, while you may not have all the answers, you have some very good questions – and plenty of time to answer them.

The Hanged Man is a signal to slow down and let things happen, to not become upset about delays, or the fruits of your labour not appearing as soon as you'd have liked. Forcing a situation to unfold on your terms and to your desired timeframe may not be the best approach. Delays can actually give you more space to understand another's point of view.

Growth takes time; enlightenment, an eternity. The Hanged Man asks you to be patient with yourself and others. Being still will allow you to gaze deeper into the mystery of 'why'.

JOURNAL PROMPTS

+ Where are you trying to force things in your current situation? Write down all the reasons you want things to happen on your schedule. Perhaps there's an external deadline, or you're worried about time running out, or being left behind. For each reason, add another line about what will happen if things unfold in their own time instead.

+ Practise patience by making time to meditate today. Once you're somewhere quiet and have found a comfortable seated position, set the timer on your phone for 20 minutes. Close your eyes and begin to extend your breathing. Make each breath extra-long, counting up to 10 with each inhale and exhale and pausing for a moment at the 'top' and 'bottom' of each breath. When you've finished, note the sensations in your body and the quality of your thoughts. How do you feel?

DEATH.

DEATH

You and your partner leave the cinema in silence and start walking home.

'What did you think of the movie?' they ask, eventually.

'It was nice,' you respond.

Then silence. Then more silence. It's not that either of you are mad. Actually, that would make things easier, because at least there would be some type of emotion. You're not sure what's wrong, but you know something isn't right. So you just keep walking.

You make it home. After sitting on the sofa for a bit with a drink, it's time for bed and perfunctory sex. When everything's over and done with, you turn away and look at the wall. You don't know why you're even in this relationship anymore. You're not sure what happened, but you've had enough. So you get up, put on your clothes and leave.

Maybe it's over. Maybe it's not.

But the way things are going right now, it has to stop.

Card number 13 of the Major Arcana often shows Death as a skeleton dressed in black armour. Its message is that something is dying and that mourning this loss cannot be avoided. Nothing that has expired is simply erased. This card reminds us that grieving is a phase to be acknowledged.

While many try to be philosophical about the Death card, reminding us that 'when one door closes, another one opens', it's hard to remember this when confronted with a loss. The visuals and the message of the card are usually intense, but they're meant to be that way. Sometimes there is no sugar-coating things. And that's okay.

Death represents an end, often signalling sudden, abrupt change (it may be one that feels like it has been a long time coming). As painful as it is necessary, you can make this card work for you by being the one who determines how you react when the change happens.

Perhaps it's the end of a childhood friendship that no longer works now you've moved away from home. The Death card suggests pulling the plug, or at least putting things on ice for a while. Maybe it's that nine-to-five that's slowly sucking your spirit? Take actions – perhaps taking the initiative and turning in your resignation will prime the universe's pump and prompt a recruiter to look at your LinkedIn profile.

The Death card reminds us that endings are inevitable. All we can control is how we close the door.

JOURNAL PROMPTS

+ What in your life is ending? This could be a physical situation, a belief or an emotional pattern. And what part of you does not want to let it go? Write down any fears that come up as you consider life 'without it'. What are you really afraid of?

+ Bring to mind something you are currently trying to manifest in your life. Could it be that you need to let something go in order to create space for it to land? Holding the vision of what you desire in your mind, journal about what comes up when you consider what may be preventing you from attaining it (again, this could be something material or a belief) and how you can let it go.

+ How can we change our attitude to death as a society? Imagine that you are on a mission to 'rebrand' this life transition and write an imaginary press release about all the good things about death. Include suggestions for how to prepare for and honour this rite of passage. How does seeing death in this way make you feel?

XIV

TEMPERANCE.

TEMPERANCE

What do you get when you mix water, lemon juice, cayenne pepper and maple syrup? You get cranky, that's what. But you're embarking on yet another 'cleanse' because you indulged in a steady diet of pizza, pasta, more pasta and more pizza the week before. You were busy and just didn't have time to eat healthy.

So now you're in the kitchen mixing up a 'quick fix'. This doesn't feel healthy either, but it's fast and you'll get results. What you could do instead, though, is chop up some veggies and make a quick, delicious stir-fry. Then, in the time it takes to do the washing up, you could plan tasty, nourishing meals for the rest of the week.

But why would you want to do that?

You need to be punished and you thrive on extremes.

After all, you're already looking forward to rewarding yourself with more pizza and pasta once you've made it through the cleanse.

Temperance is card number 14 of the Major Arcana and usually shows an angelic figure standing at the edge of a body of water, pouring a liquid between two cups. A sun on the angel's forehead shines a heavenly light on their task, blessing them with the alchemical knowledge needed to keep the water properly mixed and flowing.

Like the Justice card, Temperance is associated with balance. But while Justice creates external balance by decree, Temperance creates internal balance by remaining calm. Temperance isn't about going to extremes to avoid or withdraw from all temptation. It's about moderation. It's also about taking two complete opposites and merging them into one unified way of being.

The Temperance card can help you to identify your extremes and to work on ways to bring them closer to centre. For example, how's your work–life balance? Are you staying late at the office and can't figure out where all your time is going? Perhaps if you could cut back on those numerous coffee breaks with your colleagues, you might be able to leave at a decent hour. Are you struggling to get back into running? Perhaps instead of clocking up 10km on the first day and then paying for it with sore muscles the next you could try starting with 5km and working your way up?

But the big question Temperance asks is: 'Why are you going to extremes? Where did you learn this behaviour? What are you compensating for?' Considering this can help us find a measured way to unlearn any exhausting all-or-nothing patterns.

JOURNAL PROMPTS

+ In what areas of life do you experience the most extreme behaviour? Perhaps it's food, exercise, dating or work. Is there part of you that 'gets off' on taking things to their limits? Write a list of the pros and cons of taking an all-or-nothing attitude to life. Notice how your body responds when you consider behaving more moderately.

+ How is all-or-nothing thinking impacting your current situation? If you are faced with a decision or find yourself agonizing over an as-yet unknown outcome, notice where your thoughts are veering into the extreme. Write some of these thoughts down (for example, 'I can either be well rested or work hard). For each one that comes up, consider an alternative that's more 'both/and' (for example, 'I can get a good amount of rest and also work hard within my capabilities').

+ What inner rules do you abide by that are actually designed to punish you for being or wanting 'too much'? At the other end of the spectrum, in what areas of life do you feel you are not or do not have 'enough'? Write out three 'too much' examples and three 'not enough' examples and consider some ways in which you could balance out your self-talk in these areas.

THE DEVIL .

THE DEVIL

Just one more, right? Just one more drink. But you said that an hour – and four gin and tonics – ago. It's not like you hide it. You're always the life of the party and have no qualms about putting a few away to have a good time. And what's wrong with a little drink now and then?

Nothing has happened because of your drinking (yet). You still get up in the morning and put in a full day. Perhaps you're not as productive as before, but no one seems to notice. Or, if they do notice, they don't mind. At least that's what you tell yourself.

The problem is that your memory isn't what it was. Did you really crawl under the tree at the office Christmas party and throw up? Yes, you did. Did you really pass out in the hallway after you made it home? Yes, you did. Did you really grab your partner in a rage and almost go too far? Sadly, yes, you did.

The Devil finds us as we reach card number 15. Usually represented by a figure who dominates the scene on the card, the Devil represents temptation and can also reflect a side of yourself that is a source of shame or embarrassment for you. Your shadow side comes into play with this card.

What's your ball and chain? Your obsession? Is it a relationship you can't let go of, even though the other person has moved on? Maybe it's how often you check your social media feeds, filling your mind with images that prove you are not 'good enough'. Or perhaps it is excessive substance use. Whatever your poison, the Devil card may signal that it's time to get some help.

But there's another side to the Devil card: it can represent certain parts of yourself that you are being asked to acknowledge and accept. Usually, your shadow side is something you keep to yourself, the part of you that may exhibit behaviours or beliefs you don't want others to see. But, as the saying goes, 'You're only as sick as your secrets.' Coming to grips with and accepting certain, perhaps uncomfortable, things about yourself lessens the power they have over you.

'And who knows?' the Devil asks you. 'Perhaps your secrets aren't really that sick after all.'

JOURNAL PROMPTS

+ Write a list of all the things you are ashamed of. Perhaps it's things you've done, thoughts you sometimes have, or even parts of your family or lineage that make you uncomfortable. Take your time with this and ritualize your space: light a candle, hold your favourite crystal and have the Devil card somewhere you can see it. When you're done, in whatever way feels appropriate to you, let yourself know that you accept and forgive yourself for everything on the list. Then burn it.

+ What addictive behaviours are you ready to let go of? If nothing immediately comes to mind, pay close attention to your thoughts and actions over the coming days and note anything you find yourself engaging in that feels like a distraction or that you know is unhealthy for you – often these are things we do almost unconsciously. Note any resistance that comes up when you 'quit'. What feelings are present in the space that's left behind?

+ Write down three things you are currently 'obsessed' with. It could be an idea, a person, or something you're considering purchasing the next time you get paid. What do you think you will feel a year from now if you 'get it'? And how will your life play out if you don't?

THE TOWER.

THE TOWER

You're not a suspicious person, but you just can't shake the feeling. Your partner has always arrived home at the same time, sticking to their usual schedule without fail. But over the past few weeks, they've been showing up at different times: sometimes a little earlier, sometimes a little later. They're also moody and anxious. And when you ask if anything's wrong, they snap at you and leave the room.

You finally figure out that there is still a slight pattern to in their behaviour. They've been late the past two Fridays in a row, so you assume that they'll be home late this Friday, too.

Perhaps that's why you are so shocked when they come home early and find you on the sofa with your lover. They've known about the affair the whole time.

The Tower, number 16 in the Major Arcana, is a jolt to the system. The card features a bolt of lightning striking a solid, stable structure. The Tower stands tall in the middle of the card, representing ideas, situations or even relationships that were thought to be sound. The bolt, a sudden shock, strikes the tower and sets it on fire. The occupants jump for their lives, not knowing if they'll survive. They're surrounded by golden sparks, the pieces of their lives and dreams being incinerated into ashes.

Why do we experience 'Tower' moments in our lives? Most of us are taught from childhood that if we work hard and lay the correct groundwork, we'll be secure, maybe even successful. So that's what we do: we go to school, work hard to get decent grades, go to university, find a job, find a partner and so on.

What we're not taught is that even when we follow all the rules and build the 'perfect' lives for ourselves, there is no guarantee of a fairy-tale ending. You might flunk out of school. You might get fired from your job. You may realize you're not happy. Your partner might cheat on you (or you on them).

When these things happen, you realize that the foundation upon which you've built your life – your 'tower' – isn't so sturdy. A racist boss, a diagnosis, unfaithfulness or just plain shitty luck can be the lightning bolt that brings everything crashing down.

The question is, what do you do in the aftermath? Do you go into perpetual mourning over what was lost, clinging to the identity of 'victim' for comfort? Or do you sift through the rubble and realize that the base of your tower was rotten to the core? If anything can be salvaged, great. If not, it's time for a fresh start. The Tower card can also represent a stressful situation that has built up to the point of becoming explosive – followed by relief.

When the Tower card shows up, it is here to help you work through a major shock to the system. Think of it as the universe's way of ripping the plaster off. The pain is sharp, but quick. And allowing air to get to the wound will help you begin to heal.

JOURNAL PROMPTS

- Think about a time when you experienced an abrupt change in your life. Is part of you still hurting from it? Perhaps you've been living a little 'smaller' as a result, fearful that it may happen again. Write a letter to this part of yourself, letting it know that, while change can be an unwelcome shock to the system, you are always supported and taken care of by the divine.

- List all the things you take for granted as 'dead certs' – both good and bad. Then, for each, note why this is not necessarily a given. For example, if you write 'Losing my job means I'll become destitute,' follow it with, 'If I lose my job, I could find a better-paid position.' When you've finished the exercise, notice if you feel any differently about the idea of sudden change.

XVII

THE STAR.

THE STAR

The tears are welling up in your eyes as you leave the bank. You've been turned down for yet another business loan. They loved your idea, but just didn't think it was viable in the current economic climate. The thing is, you've already left your job and maxed out your credit cards, because part of you still believes you can run your own business. But how?

As you reach into your bag for your keys, your hand touches something inside that feels like a bracelet. It's your grandmother's watch. You were supposed to take it to be repaired weeks ago, but forgot about it. A memory surfaces: your grandma wearing the watch as she made you dinner. Even on a fixed income, her food always tasted like a gourmet feast.

She made a way out of no way.

You look at the watch and put it on. It's dull and broken.

But it's the reminder you need to keep going.

The Star card, number 17, brings hope following the Tower. The card normally shows a person kneeling at the edge of a pond with two jugs of water. They pour water from one jug into the pond. With the other jug, they water the grass on the bank. A large star shines above the person. Eight smaller stars surround it. This is an extremely positive card. It denotes 'hope'. It tells you to look up and to keep moving forwards. You may not know which direction to go in, but the Star does.

Think of the Star card as the calm after the storm. It brings space to regroup and to remember why you started off on your journey in the first place. The card asks you to dive into your pool of consciousness. To go deep to find your faith again. When you emerge, the Star will be there to show you the way forward.

After a disappointment or derailment, we all need something or someone to restore our faith and remind us that all is not lost. Not faith in a religious sense, but a universal one. Faith that somehow, things are going to work out. But in order to act on this, we must also allow ourselves to be led; to turn off the GPS of our thoughts and follow the North Star of our intuition.

The Star card carries the message to look inside, to go deep and to remember how and why you started on your path. It is calling to the university student who just screwed up yet another exam; to the parent of a longed-for child who won't stop screaming her head off in her cot; to anybody who finds themselves lost and questioning why they are even here.

Allow the Star to bring forth a talisman, a memory or a flash of insight that reminds you of the 'why' of whatever you're facing. Meditate on this and keep it with you. Make it your own personal North Star.

JOURNAL PROMPTS

+ Take a moment to remind yourself of the greater 'why' behind your current situation. List any frustrations that are present, along with any desired outcomes that feel out of reach. For each thing you write down, ask yourself: 'Why?' *Why* is this making me angry? *Why* am I attached to that? *Why* am I putting in all this work when things aren't going my way?'

+ Who are your role models? Bring to mind three to five people who embody the traits that you aspire to and list all the things you admire about them. This could be what they've achieved, what they represent or the way they respond to certain situations. How would they behave in your current circumstances?

+ What does 'faith' mean to you? Write about a time when you had no choice but to trust that things would work out. What was challenging about this? What was the outcome? What did you learn about yourself and the universe in the process?

THE MOON.

THE MOON

Years ago, when you were majoring in film at a university in your hometown in the southern US, you had to shoot a scene in a cemetery. Because of logistics and regulations, your team had to park their trucks all the way on the other side of a large field, which was across from where you were shooting. You used the field as a shortcut when unloading the trucks.

As you ran back and forth, carrying tripods, cameras and lights, you kept getting a weird feeling in middle of the field. You'd stand there, with the sensation of being sent some kind of message. 'What am I supposed to know about this place?' you asked yourself (and the universe). But you didn't have time to find the answer. You had a film to shoot.

You found your answer about six months later, when news reports came out that the unmarked graves of 300 enslaved African Americans – your ancestors – had been discovered in that very field.

The Moon, card number 18, reminds you to check in with your subconscious. It asks you to sort through the messages that have piled up during your day (or lifetime) and are waiting to be delivered. The Moon card in the RWS deck shows a wolf and a dog howling at the sky as the moon, this familiar yet unknown entity, rises over the horizon.

There's something beautifully unnerving about taking a walk in the forest in the deep of night. During the day, you take notice of what you can see. At night, you take notice of what you *can't* see. Is something moving behind that tree? What was that sound? Should I go closer or take a different path?

But now, your other senses come to your aid. The scent of pine brings comfort as you remember the stoic presence of the trees. You hear the water of a stream flowing, a familiar sound. The sensation of your breath in your body reminds you to breathe deeply and stay calm. And then, when your eyes finally adjust, you can see the night-time magic of the forest.

Similarly, the Moon invites you into a deeper relationship with the unknown parts of yourself – or, rather, what you *think* is unknown. Your subconscious is the link to your inner mysteries and you have more access to it than you think.

For example, what's the first thing you do when you wake up? Do you remember your dreams? Writing them down is a simple way of capturing the subconscious messages that arose while you slept and always brings deeper insight.

You can also use the energy of the Moon card to help you see what you're missing as you go about your day. For example, try listening to the tone and register of someone's voice and not just the words they say during conversations. Can you tell if they're stressed? Confused? Perhaps hiding something?

Let the Moon help you retrieve the messages your subconscious leaves behind.

JOURNAL PROMPTS

+ Many of us are afraid of the dark. Challenge yourself to feel more comfortable in the 'unseen' realms by turning off all the lights in your home this evening and going to bed in the pitch black. What fears are present? If any panic arises, settle yourself by deepening your breathing, taking long, slow inhales and exhales. Notice what thoughts appear when you allow your mind and body to settle into the dark.

+ Bring to mind a time you received a 'message' from your subconscious, seemingly out of nowhere. Perhaps it was a memory that surfaced, giving you some insight into a current situation, or an intuitive urge to stay away from a certain person. What did you learn about yourself? How can you create more space in your life to listen to your inner knowing?

THE SUN .

THE SUN

There's a job on a professional networking platform that you'd love to go for, but you know for an absolute fact that it's not the right job for you. It's not that you're not qualified. You know you are. It's just that the job would be so… big.

You'd be so… seen. Which is something you've always been afraid of. You tried it when you were younger, when you recited one of your poems at the annual school talent show. Your classmates laughed you off the stage and you were heartbroken. But that was then and this is now. So you decide to give the job a shot and send in your application.

A few days later, you get a call from the company's HR department. The representative says they're not sure if you're the right fit for that particular position. From looking at your application, they'd like to consider you for something even higher up within the company.

Card number 19, the Sun, is one of the most positive cards. It is usually depicted with a bright, glowing star in the middle, exuding happiness, confidence and lifted spirits. This is the card of openness, of being proud of who you are and what you've achieved. It's about truth and being free.

The Sun card has one simple task for you: rejoice! Rejoice that you found that parking space, that you kept your cool when you had every right to lose it, that you are here on this planet. Bask in the glow of your worth and remember that life itself is a gift. The Sun card suggests that you try to inject positive energy into your endeavours, even if you don't feel up to it at the moment. There needs to be space for the good news to land.

If you've been playing small, this card is a rallying cry to step into your power. And introverts, take note; you don't need an audience to do this. You can celebrate yourself *by* yourself.

If you have a tendency to negate or ignore your achievements, this card showing up says it's time to stop and smell the roses. To pause, stop pushing and take inventory on just how far you've come and all that you have accomplished in getting here.

This card wants you to honour all that you embody as a beautiful, talented and innovative human being. To know that you deserve success, love and whatever other great things the universe has in store for you. But remember one thing; you must also believe that you are worthy and be ready to receive. So spread your arms wide and accept the gifts.

JOURNAL PROMPTS

+ Write all your positive qualities on different sticky notes and stick them around your home. But wait: why does the idea of this bring up any discomfort about 'loving yourself' or inviting negative comments from others? Where do you think this tendency to play down your gifts comes from? Journal about any feelings or doubts that come up.

+ Make a playlist of songs that you can't help singing along to and which always lift your spirits. Take your time thinking about the list over the coming days before you actually compile it on your music app, revisiting different times in your life when you felt confident and celebratory. What songs were playing on repeat for you then? When you listen to them, pay attention to the lyrics. What's the message?

+ In what areas of life do you tend to suffer from low self-esteem? And in what areas do you feel most confident and self-assured? Note down a few observations for each and consider the formative experiences that led to you feeling this way: what made you feel unsure about speaking in public? Why are you so confident about your cooking skills? Now have the 'confident' you offer words of encouragement to your 'unsure' self. What do you want them to know?

JUDGEMENT.

JUDGEMENT

The guilt has followed you for years. You and your closest colleague from your previous job were both frustrated and dreamed of getting out. More than once, you perused the online job listings together over lunch, looking at various positions. You each even promised to find a way to take the other along if one of you found a new gig first.

And then you got offered a new job. A fabulous management position in which you could create your own team, which you did. The problem was that your old colleague, still toiling away at your previous company, just didn't fit the new work culture you were now part of. Or so you decided. They emailed and called, remembering the promise you had both made. But you never picked up the phone or responded to their messages. You basically ghosted them when you could have hired them.

The last you heard, they'd finally left the company to retrain and go into another field entirely. You're happy for them, but the guilt still remains. You pick up your phone. If you can't offer them a job, you can at least offer an apology.

The Judgement card can trigger a lot of anxiety. Number 20 in the deck, it usually shows a winged figure hovering in the sky, blowing a trumpet to wake up the dead souls in the graveyard below. As we would imagine, Judgement is seen as a signal to reckon with past actions and to ask forgiveness. But when it comes to making amends, this doesn't necessarily mean apologizing to someone else. Sometimes we are our own harshest critics and punishing ourselves and holding on to self-judgement can weigh us down. Forgiving yourself for your perceived 'wrongdoings' lightens your load and allows you to judge yourself – and others – more favourably. Forgiving yourself also paves the way for any person you may have wronged to forgive you, too.

Judgement can also help you make a decision on an issue that's been hovering around for a while. The sound of the angel's trumpet can be a wake-up call, urging you to address a situation head on, especially if you've been avoiding it because of the possibility of guilt connected to it.

In this vein, a final expression of the card's energy can be a call to follow your heart. Do you feel pulled towards a different path? Is there a change in your life you need to make, no matter how others may feel about it? This change could be mundane or spiritual. It could be simple or complex. Whatever it is, the Judgement card signals that this is the right time.

JOURNAL PROMPTS

+ Take an inventory of your past 'wrongs'. This may include ways you behaved poorly towards others, or times you dissed yourself! For one, consider what it would take to make it 'right'. Could it be offering a heart-felt apology? Making a donation to a particular cause? Or perhaps forgiving yourself? Commit to working through your list in the coming weeks and months.

+ What have you been putting off for fear of judgement from others? Write down all the things you think they'll have to say about it: perhaps that you're selfish, or that it's not your place to take whatever action you are feeling called to take. Now imagine lovingly responding to each of these critiques, acknowledging their concerns and letting them know that your intention is not to cause any harm. In this process, consider how you might proceed in a way that takes everybody's needs and feelings into account.

+ Is there somebody in your life you need to forgive? Bring any resentments about your situation to mind and consider the cost to your time and energy in holding on to them. Forgiveness doesn't have to mean being a doormat and letting people walk all over you. Use this as an opportunity to practise setting better boundaries and then let go and turn the other cheek.

THE WORLD.

THE WORLD

You have arrived. After many stops, starts and detours, life has finally brought you to where you want to be. You have survived years of mistakes and missteps. You have listened, you have learned and you have been tested.

The road has been paved with moments of joy, heartbreak, fear and sometimes even sheer terror. You were tempted to give in, but you kept going. And something happened along the way: you realized that the perfect job, house or partner wasn't what you needed to be happy. You also realized that there was no such thing as the perfect job, house or partner.

All you needed, all along, was you. And the experiences your soul came here to have to make you whole.

Are you finished? Not by a long shot. But are you now equipped with the wisdom and the tools to embark on the next stage of your life? You bet.

We reach the end of the Major Arcana with the World card, number 21. The card of realization, of achievement and of contentment. It usually shows a figure centred in the middle of a wreath, with mystical beasts looking on from each corner.

The World card helps us celebrate crossing the finish line and successfully passing the tests of the Major Arcana. The experiences we've had along the way have helped us learn and grow, preparing us to 'graduate' to the next stage of our lives. The laurel wreath depicted on the card in the RWS deck can even be read as 'crowning' your next rebirth, as you push your newly ascended self through to a higher level.

This card showing up shows that the work you've put into your growth has paid off. You are in communion with the Universe and it shows in your words and deeds. You are a positive influence on those around you. You are loved and you are love.

If you have a tendency to negate or minimize your experiences, or have a hard time celebrating your accomplishments, visualize yourself in the middle of this card. It shows your celestial graduation. This card is also a potent antidote to impostor syndrome. No one is waiting to call you out; no one is going to take away your success. You've earned it.

Allow yourself to feel proud of this achievement. That other shoe you're waiting on to drop? It's a glass slipper. And when it lands, you'll see that it fits you perfectly.

JOURNAL PROMPTS

+ Think back over the past 'season' of your life. What are the biggest lessons you have learned? Write down five to ten things you know now that you could not have known 'back then'. Now look forward to the challenges that lie ahead. Write down five to ten things you would like to discover the answers to, about the world and about yourself.

+ What goals did you have for yourself one year ago, five years ago and ten years ago? List as many as you can remember and, for each one, write about whether you feel you have achieved it or not and how you feel about this. If any of your goals fell by the wayside, what did this make space for in your life instead? If you did achieve a goal, did it bring the sense of satisfaction that you wanted?

+ Choose a 'wise elder' role model to accompany you on the next phase in your life journey. This could be a historical figure, somebody you know or someone in the public eye. How do they embody and share their wisdom? What life experiences made them so wise? Find an image of them and keep it on your altar, your phone or your desktop. Check in with them any time you feel you need to.

THE
MINOR
ARCANA

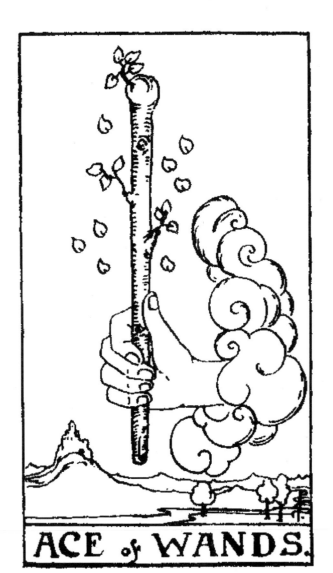

ACE of WANDS.

ACE OF WANDS

You and your buddies are watching the news on TV. Stories about the latest slew of conflicts and strife flash across the screen. You feel absolutely helpless. As you listen to one soundbite after the other from diplomats and politicians, you think to yourself, 'Why in the world can't we put negotiations in the hands of the people affected by the conflict?'

'Why can't we crowdsource peace?' you say out loud.

Everyone turns and looks at you.

Then comes the reply: 'Wait. Why can't we?'

The following two hours are filled with sticky notes, napkins, notebook paper... and ideas. The next thing you know, you and your friends have put together a proposal for an online peace platform. You have no idea how it happened, but it did. And it feels good. It's all a crazy idea on paper at the moment. But at least it's a start.

The Ace of Wands is the first card of the Wands suit and represents an idea that seems to spring forth from nowhere. It trumpets the arrival of the fiery Wands energy and the heat of creation. The Ace of Wands card usually depicts a hand holding a wand as it emerges from the sky.

This card signals invention, innovation and entrepreneurial spirit. It says, 'Got an idea? Go for it.' You may pull this card when you feel a call to get creative, but you're not sure why. Perhaps a message is trying to come forth through a magic portal (or the television!). Open yourself to innovation. Drop all expectations of what the process or the outcome should look like. If you can dream it, you can do it.

The Ace of Wands asks you to honour your creative flashes, those crazy ideas that couldn't possibly work – until they do. Keep in mind that there's no need for your plan to be fully formed right now. This is just the beginning.

JOURNAL PROMPTS

+ Before you go to sleep tonight, 'request' a dream that gives you a clue about what to create with your life next. You could write this request out in your journal, speak it out loud or just say it in your head. Then, upon waking, write down as much as you can remember about what you dreamed. What seed is being planted?

+ Write down five ideas or innovations you wish you had come up with. For each one, consider the creative mind behind it and get curious about the process that brought the idea to fruition. Is it an example of creative problem-solving? Is it an expression of the person's talents or specific skill set, or perhaps an homage to their lineage? Think about which elements of yourself and your unique life experience are ready to be made manifest in a similar way.

TWO OF WANDS

Your boss is explaining your idea to the board. And he's completely screwing it up. Due to company hierarchy, it's his job to present the concept, not yours. It's also his job to sound confident about it. He doesn't.

You were only able to show him the new storyboards this morning. He'd been too busy until then. The idea could take things in a whole new direction, using actual product-users to tell their stories instead of the brand's expensive celebrity ambassador. Costs would be lower and the campaign would be more realistic.

'So, where is our brand ambassador in this?' asks the CEO.

'Oh! Uh... we'll just CGI him in during post-production. He'll ride in on his motorcycle, hop off and deliver the tag line directly to the camera,' says your boss.

That's not on the storyboard.

Everyone stares at your boss in disbelief. He looks at you.

That's when you push back your chair, stand and ask: 'May I?'

The Two of Wands calls for you to stand in your power, believe in yourself and your ideas and 'own the room'. It uses the fiery Wands energy to spark self-confidence and the faith that you've got what it takes, even before you take a step towards your goal. The Two of Wands card usually shows a person holding a globe, which represents plans and potential. One wand is held in their left hand; another leans against the wall to their right. The person is gazing at the landscape below.

The card represents being brave and bold when others can't – or won't. It signals situations in which you need to take control and convince others to consider a different direction. The Two of Wands speaks to a potential that perhaps only you can see – but it's one which you can also feel and almost taste. It's about not only being able to see the big picture, but also knowing which brushes and paint will be needed and the right type of canvas to use.

The Two of Wands brings a boost of confidence to help you execute an idea. It says that you know the risks and are willing to take them. It puts the power of creativity in your hands.

JOURNAL PROMPTS

✦ Where have you been playing small and not asserting yourself, out of fear that it's 'not your place'? Now visualize yourself speaking up and imagine a positive chain of events unfolding as a result. Where do you end up? If nothing comes forward, bring to mind a past situation when you wanted to contribute, but failed to throw your hat into the ring. How might things have gone differently had you put your ideas forward then?

✦ When considering how to move forwards in your current situation, which tools do you have to hand to help you make your move? These tools could be your innate talents or a specific skill set you have mastered; they could include your research capabilities, or your network of contacts and allies. With all these resources to hand, what are you waiting for?

THREE OF WANDS

Your mother holds your university acceptance letter in her hands. You knew there was only a small chance of getting in, but you applied anyway – to a university 1,200 miles away.

'I know it's far away,' you say, with a smile. 'But weren't you the one who always said "aim high"?'

'Yes – I said "aim *high*". Not "aim east and head towards the Atlantic",' she says, as she put her arm around you.

You've taken care of her for years as she battled drug addiction.

She has been home from the treatment programme for six months now. Taking responsibility has never been her strong point, but this time feels different. It's like she knew she had to leave her old life behind for good and find professional support. And by addressing her drug use at last, she has finally been able to look forwards and see the possibilities for your life and hers.

L ike many of the cards in this suit, the Three of Wands brings an extremely positive message. It often shows a figure with its back to us, looking out at the sea. The figure holds one wand in their right hand, while two more are positioned behind them.

This card is linked to having foresight, planning ahead and being positive about the future. It wants you to get a bird's-eye view of the situation so you can map your way to success.

Like the Two of Wands, this card is associated with self-confidence, but it also speaks to the confidence that others place in you. For this reason, the Three of Wands also represents support: people having your back and you having theirs. When it's time, confident in your own abilities and knowing that you have the backing you need, you'll be able to take the lead on the journey without hesitation.

Meditate on this card to help you to clearly see the path to your goal and to find the strength to seize the moment and set off, confidently, towards it.

JOURNAL PROMPTS

+ Think about something you would like to manifest in your life. It could be a project, a situation or something you would like to see transformed in our wider society. Now write down a list of all the things needed to bring this about. Include the practicalities, the mental adjustments and the support you may need from others. Is the idea of this desire becoming a reality really so far-fetched?

+ When you think about your future, what do you see? We often have an idea of how we believe our lives will 'play out', even if this isn't something we're consciously aware of. List all the things that come up when you focus on this. For all the 'positives', consider what actions you can begin to take now to help bring them to fruition. For any 'negatives', question where these beliefs come from. What could you put in place now to begin to rewrite this script?

FOUR OF WANDS

They knew you wouldn't plan anything to commemorate the finalization of your divorce. After three years of back and forth, you sent one short email to your soon-to-be ex that put a stop to the games: 'What do I have to sign to get you out of my life?'

No one could believe what you did next. You signed away your rights to almost everything: the house, the cars, the bank accounts, the lifestyle.

But it was worth it. You can finally put the screaming, the shouting and the abuse behind you.

So what's left? Everything that you can fit into your new one-room apartment, which isn't much. But the most precious thing in your possession is your sanity. Your peace. You are free.

Three friends have supported you through it all, sticking with you after everyone else had fallen to the wayside. And here you all are, sitting on the floor in the middle of your tiny new abode. You join hands and look at each other, smiling, then scream for joy. You did it!

The Four of Wands carries themes of freedom, breaking free, celebration and a sense of finally being able to breathe. The card usually shows four wands draped with fruit and vines. The number four represents a stable structure, literally and metaphorically, and the Four of Wands signals security and a 'safe space' blessed by friends. This card signals not just the achievement of a goal itself, but also the celebration marking this moment in your life. It gives you permission to let go and give it up to spirit.

Do you have a difficult time celebrating your personal breakthroughs and evolutions? Is there resistance when your friends, family or colleagues reflect on how far you've come and tell you that it's okay to give yourself a break? The Four of Wands has the energy to help you find ways to honour and commemorate the achievements that free you from the shackles of the past and spur you onwards.

Whether with a big ol' party with dozens of friends or an intimate dinner with a loved one, this card is a reminder to put a big, beautiful bow on your success and celebrate your successes and how far you've come.

JOURNAL PROMPTS

- When was the last time you felt like you had a personal breakthrough? Perhaps it was quitting a habit that was holding you back, ending a toxic relationship or doing the work to turn over a new leaf in your career. How did you celebrate? If the answer is 'I didn't', then consider a way to commemorate your success in the coming days. It's never too late to mark these important moments.

- Bring to mind a situation in which you feel trapped. What would it take to 'free' yourself? This may seem like a daunting task – and there's no need to do anything rash today. For now, take a few moments in meditation to conjure the feeling of freedom in your body. Breathe deeply into the sensation of having more room to move in your life. Carry this feeling with you as inspiration for your path forwards.

FIVE OF WANDS

'Whac-A-Mole' is an arcade game in which plastic moles pop out of their holes one by one. You have to bang each one of the moles on the head with a heavy foam mallet before it disappears to score a point. As soon as you whack one mole on the head, forcing it to retreat into its hole, another will pop up. The catch is that the game gets faster as you go along.

Some days feel like that, don't they? If it's not one thing, it's another. And another. And another.

You've just got to work after dropping your youngest off at school (late) and you get a call that they've thrown up in class. You have a meeting in ten minutes and you've just spilled coffee on your blouse. And now a couple of your colleagues are walking up to your desk; they have issues with slides 11, 37 and 47 of the 70-slide presentation you stayed up until 2am working on.

You're close to losing your cool and having a meltdown. But what will this achieve?

The Five of Wands represents the daily hassles of life: the things that, by themselves, don't seem to be a big deal, but when they happen one after the other, finding your way through the day gets hard. The Five of Wands card usually depicts five figures wielding poles as if they're practising combat. This card signals irritation, pettiness, egos and futile contests. It reflects situations where we may find ourselves arguing for the sake of it, or just acting petulantly. But, on the flipside, it can also represent healthy competition and debate.

Meditate on the Five of Wands to help you discern which 'hassle' is worth your attention. Is going back and forth with your colleagues about the location of the recycling container a good use of your energy? Or is it better to go back and forth with your local authority about the city's recycling plan overall? Only you get to decide what's worth getting worked up over.

JOURNAL PROMPTS

+ List all the things that are currently irritating you, big and small. If you knew that this was your last week on Earth, what would you focus on resolving? With this in mind, go back over your list and try to simply 'let go' of any tension or anxiety about the 'small stuff'. Is it really worth the aggro in the long run?

+ Is there somebody in your life who always seems to find a way to get under your skin? Take a moment to consider what it is about their manner, the way they act or how they talk to you, that you find so irritating. What do they trigger in you? Put yourselves in the shoes of an outside observer. What would this person have to say about the situation that you are unable to see?

SIX OF WANDS

You've never been a good student. For some reason, you've always struggled to pay attention to the teacher and find the other students a distraction. It seems that every time you allowed your mind to float through the window, over the football field and into that amazingly free space called your imagination, Mrs Porter's stern voice would break through, snapping you back to reality.

She called you stupid. And so did your classmates.

Although moving to a new school has been challenging, this one has a special programme for young people who think like you. And, hey, some of them even look like you, too.

It takes just one test to change everyone's minds. You score so highly that there is no room for discussion about the results.

Who knew? You were brilliant all along!

You just needed the right type of stimulation, in the right type of environment.

Victory and vindication are two words associated with the Six of Wands. The card normally shows a person riding a horse and holding a wand. Five more wands can be seen at the bottom of the card. This card suggests you've been heading along a path that not many have understood. Perhaps it was a new way of doing something, or a creative project in which no one else could see the beauty. You might have felt very alone in this, nervous and unsure of yourself. Nevertheless, you persisted. And you're now on the path to redemption.

Meditate on the Six of Wands to boost your self-confidence, especially when those who believe in you are few. Imagine your friends and family – and even your naysayers – lining your road to victory. But be careful; you haven't made it to the finish line just yet. Keep going, keep putting in the work and stay true to yourself, until you reach your destination.

JOURNAL PROMPTS

+ Bring to mind a time when you felt like an outsider because you chose to go with your instincts rather than follow the crowd. If this is something you would *never* do, imagine how it would feel to go out on a limb in this way; would it be frightening, or freeing? Now write down all the qualities needed to stay true to yourself when it means choosing the unconventional path. How can you begin to cultivate these qualities for yourself?

+ Write about somebody you admire who always does things their own way. What is it you value about their attitude, their ideas and their contribution? It could be somebody in your life, or a famous person you admire from afar. Now consider what area of your life could benefit from you embodying some of their confidence and self-belief. How would this shift the situation?

SEVEN OF WANDS

Apparently, some people can pay their bills with this magical currency called 'exposure'.

You're not one of them.

But when a famous singer notices your artwork on Instagram and contacts you, you are more than flattered. They love what you are doing and want to support you, so they offer to place one of your pieces in a scene in their upcoming video. The only catch? They'll be paying for the artwork with 'exposure'.

Their representative, and even your friends, tell you that other artists would kill to be offered this chance. You ponder this dilemma for days. At the same time, you're also thinking about all the bills you have to pay. This could be your big break. Having your work show up in this star's video could make you hot property.

But it could also set a dangerous precedent – for you and for your fellow artists, too. Someone needs to let the celebrity know that promising nothing but exposure is not okay.

That someone is you.

Bravery is the key word for the Seven of Wands, which usually shows a figure standing on a hill, holding a wand and using it to bat back six wands below them. This card represents taking a stand, going for what you want and fighting for what you believe in, no matter the odds.

The Seven of Wands signals taking a very strong position and doing so knowing, without a doubt, that you're right. But here's the thing about the Seven of Wands: yes, the card can mean standing up for a cause or movement, but its real power comes through when you use its energy to stand up for *yourself*.

When you pull this card, use it to shore up your courage in the face of pressure from all sides. Trust that the strength of your convictions will see you through.

JOURNAL PROMPTS

+ What stops you from standing up for yourself? Is it fear of rejection? An aversion to conflict? People-pleasing tendencies? Think about a situation in your life where you've been staying quiet and/or playing the role of doormat and write about all the ways this is holding you (and others) back. Knowing what's at stake, can you think of one small way you can take a stand for what you know to be true?

+ Where did you learn that it's better to 'put up and shut up'? Consider all the influences in your life – such as your family, education or society at large – that may have created any negative views you might hold about people speaking up. What are some of the descriptors that come to mind when you think about people speaking up? For each thing you write down, question whether this is actually true.

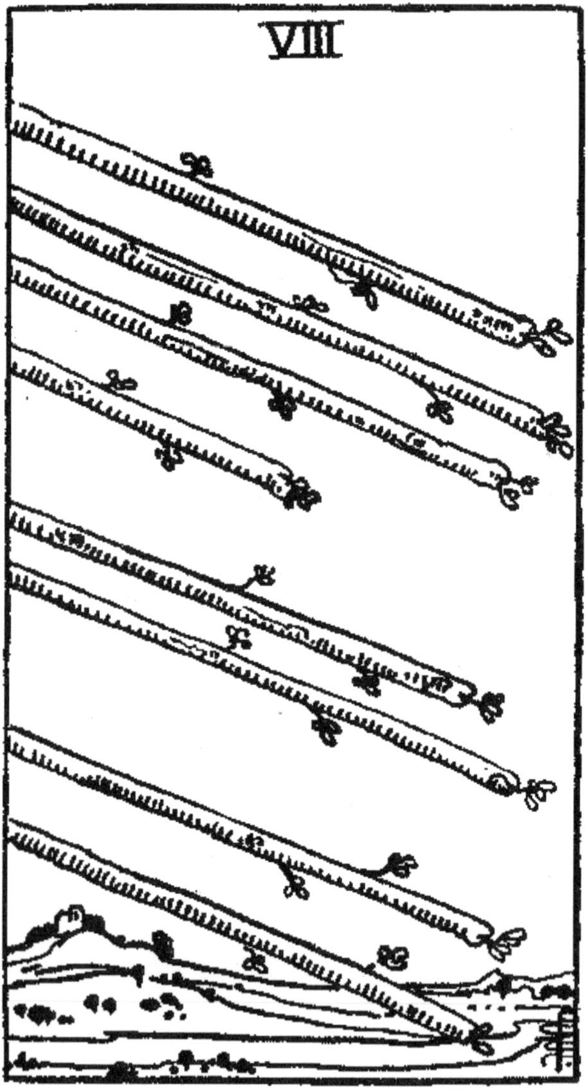
VIII

EIGHT OF WANDS

You've had the biggest crush on this person since university. For years, you worshipped them from afar. But after you both graduated, that was that. Until your class reunion.

You heard years ago that they'd got married, so you have no expectations at all when you walk up and say: 'Hi! How are you?'

'Oh hey there!' they say. 'Nice to see you again after all these years!'

After a few minutes of playing 'whatever happened to…', you ask: 'And how's the family?'

'Oh everyone's fine. The kids are fine. The ex is fine.'

'Um. The ex?'

So, what are you waiting for?

If you're waiting on a sign to act, the Eight of Wands fits the bill. This card represents speed, movement, enlightenment from above – an 'Aha!' moment that asks to be quickly acted upon. The card is usually depicted with eight wands barrelling down to earth, from left to right.

The Eight of Wands carries a message of urgency: 'Set things in motion now. Not tomorrow. Now'. It's your cue to move, to make 'it' happen, whatever 'it' is. Just get on with it and get it over and done with. It can also ask you to bring something to an end that's been languishing away.

This card can also reflect the energy of actual messages or signals that are making their way to you. If you've been expecting news or results, this card asks you to prepare for their arrival.

The Eight of Wands carries the energy you need when 'something' needs to happen in order to bring a situation out of stagnation. Is there something hanging in the balance? Perhaps a project that's stuck in the 'idea' phase? Or a tiny hint that a potential relationship may be blossoming? Hurry up and grab hold of the Eight of Wands energy and see where it takes you.

JOURNAL PROMPTS

- In the coming days, listen closely for a message from your intuition. Unlike the ego voice, which chatters away incessantly, the intuitive voice will deliver its insights quickly and then disappear again. Pay extra attention to any 'hits' you get while in the energy of the Eight of Wands and do not hesitate to act on them quickly.

- What are you procrastinating about? Bring to mind a situation where you have been stalling, unsure of which way to go, and list the pros and cons of taking whatever feels like the most aligned action. With these pros and cons in mind, ask yourself: if you had only 24 hours to act, or you'd lose the opportunity forever, what would you do?

NINE OF WANDS

Trust has to be earned. But it's hard for anyone to earn yours, because you've had to fight your way to where you are today. And that fight involved a lot of hurt.

This hurt has affected how you look at every aspect of your life: you won't apply for a job, because you know you won't get it; you refuse to show interest in the neighbour who's been trying to catch your eye, because you're sure they'll ghost you; and you refuse to cry in front of anyone, or even when you're alone, because you see it as a sign of weakness.

With these barriers in place, you continue to build a strong fence around you so nothing and no one gets in. But this also means that you can't get out.

It's draining to form and hold on to a world view based on hurt. And now, as you sit in your apartment, alone, you realize how tired you are.

Could it be that asking for help, or even just sharing some of what's going on, would lessen the load a little? Maybe knocking on your neighbour's door, just to say 'Hi,' wouldn't be such a bad idea after all.

The Nine of Wands reflects our painful battles and their after-effects. It understands the lure of closing ourselves off from the world when we have sustained wounds along the way. The card sometimes shows a person supporting themselves with a wand. A fence made of eight more wands is behind them. The person seems wary of something. The Nine of Wands appears when you want to say, 'Go away' – and prompts you to delve deeper into why.

Are you on the defensive all the time because of past experiences? Do the situations and people around you warrant the perpetual side-eye? The Nine of Wands invites you to question these feelings. You don't have to let your guard down entirely, only enough so you can see what's friend or foe.

JOURNAL PROMPTS

+ Write about a time in the past when you felt you were taken advantage of: perhaps your trust was abused or you were left feeling used. Be gentle with yourself as you bring these memories forth and let yourself know that it's safe to go there. You are safe now. What do you wish that past-self had known in order to be able to better protect themselves? Promise them that you will never let it happen again and let them know it's safe to go on living in the meantime.

+ The next time you sit down to meditate, visualize a transparent force field encircling your whole body. You can 'fill' this bubble with any colour you like and give it whatever texture feels good to you. Now imagine there are tiny holes in it, which will let in all the oxygen you need, as well as any nourishing, positive and supportive energy from your surroundings. Call on this force field any time you feel threatened, or when you need an extra layer of protection in the world.

TEN OF WANDS

The plan for you to take over the family store has been in place for years. From the time you could barely see over the counter, you've been stocking shelves and running the cash register. And as you're the oldest, it'll also be up to you to make sure your siblings are trained and employed in the business in some way. Very soon, the store – and the responsibility that comes with it   will be yours.

As your dad's retirement day gets closer, you find yourself getting more and more stressed, to the point you actually become ill. Perhaps part of that stress is about your upcoming wedding to your childhood sweetheart, who really is a nice person, but – well, something just doesn't feel right anymore.

For as long as you can remember, you've always done what you were supposed to do and lived the life you were supposed to live. But this is beginning to feel like a weight around your neck.

No, you don't want to spend your life lording over the corner shop with the perfect spouse and the cookie-cutter family.

What you really want to do is sing.

The Ten of Wands asks an important question: 'How much of what you're carrying really belongs to you?' This card often shows a person whose arms are loaded down with ten wands. Their posture is bent as they try to walk with the weight of the load they're carrying.

Perhaps you, too, are physically overburdened. Stressed. Loaded down. Or is it that you've taken on others' ideas of how things 'should be' without thinking about what you actually want or need?

The Ten of Wands may signal that you're literally taking on way too much and carrying more than your fair share. But another facet of this card also speaks to old ideas and ways of thinking that have been passed down the generations and which you are unwittingly carrying into the present. The overall message of this card is to lighten your load. It's time to drop what doesn't belong to you, so you can embrace freedom and find the energy to follow your own path.

JOURNAL PROMPTS

+ Write a list of all the things you currently have 'on your plate'. Did you purposefully place each thing there, or were some loaded on while you weren't looking? Rate each item on a scale of one to five, with five being something that's a high priority for you and one being something you are begrudgingly carrying to the point of resenting it. Now look at the low-priority items on your list. What are you ready to strike off the list completely?

+ Consider which beliefs you hold to be 'true' that do not actually belong to you. Who did you inherit them from? And what 'weight' do they carry in your life? Could that weight be holding you back? Write down one of these beliefs and consider how you could edit it so that it lines up with what your own lived experience has taught you. Can you feel the weight beginning to lift?

PAGE of WANDS.

PAGE OF WANDS

You can't expect the same passion from a marriage after ten years as it had in the beginning. Passion is often replaced by a certain type of comfort that grows as a partnership matures. Is this wrong? Of course not. Can it be boring? Hell yes.

You love your spouse so much. And you're actually still turned on by them. It's just that... well, you'd like to try something new.

Anything new.

You look at their sweet face snuggling against the pillow next to you as they doze off after a long day. There used to be a time you would both would doze off together after a long night between the sheets.

But there's hope.

You get up, go to the chest of drawers and open the top one. Tucked away in the back is something you bought a few weeks ago; a new lingerie set. You put it on. Sure, it's a tad frilly and not the most comfortable, but hopefully it'll be off soon.

You walk to your spouse's side of the bed and whisper.

'Hey. Wake up.'

The Page of Wands signals creativity, fun, passion and play. It offers a chance for discovery and adventure. The card normally shows a young person standing in the middle of a vast landscape and holding a wand. They're gazing upon it with curiosity.

The Page, much like a young child, looks at the world with big, wide eyes of wonder, ready to seek out ways to manifest whatever they desire. They know, in their heart of hearts, that those pillows stacked up in the middle of the living room form an impenetrable fort that will stand for centuries. Over there, in that cupboard, lies the portal to a magical kingdom.

The Page of Wands asks: 'Are you stuck in a rut? Are you ready for a little fun?' Use the energy of this card when you need to look at an issue with fresh eyes and excitement again.

JOURNAL PROMPTS

+ Try to see your current situation through the eyes of a younger, more innocent and less jaded version of yourself. For a moment, imagine that you have never been 'burned' and therefore have no reason to fear things going wrong again. If you were able to trust that everything would work out in your favour and that only fun times and adventure lay ahead, what actions would you take next?

- List all the ways in which you like to have fun. If the list feels short (which is very normal), include activities you have enjoyed in the past and no longer have time for, due to busy schedules and 'grown-up' responsibilities. Now look at your calendar for the coming weeks and make space for you to engage in a few of these activities. How does it feel to know that 'fun' has a place on your to-do list?

KNIGHT of WANDS.

KNIGHT OF WANDS

It's the search for excitement that keeps you going. Darting from one project to another without finishing the first, and jumping from one relationship to the next without ever achieving real intimacy. Each day – no, each minute – brings a new adventure for you. You run from one experience to the next and then the next.

Your charisma fills up a room and you're always the life and soul of the party. But what are you running from? What is it about your life and your surroundings that scares you so much that you continue to resist standing still? Resist falling in love? Resist putting down roots?

You can only run around for so long, and travel so far, before you find there's nowhere left to go – and that you're too tired to care anymore.

The Knight of Wands signals passion and zest. They are dynamic with a capital 'D'. The card usually depicts a Knight in armour, holding a wand in their right hand and riding a horse.

This card blends the speed of the Knight with the fiery energy of Wands. The result is a sexy, spiritual, Roman candle of a vibe, that can propel a plan, event or any type of situation to incredible heights – temporarily. The Knight of Wands symbolizes our personal 'blaze of glory'.

Like the other court cards in the Wands family, the Knight is self-confident. The difference is that the Knight may be a little *too* self-confident sometimes. They may start a journey at full speed, not realizing that their energy isn't limitless.

Meditate on the Knight of Wands when you need the energy to make a strong, confident start; when you just need enough of a boost to get you to cruising speed. But remember that it takes stamina to stay the course. Don't wear yourself out.

JOURNAL PROMPTS

+ Is there an area in your life where you're in danger of burning out? Besides physical and mental exhaustion, tell-tale signs include waning enthusiasm for a project, procrastination and self-doubt. It could be the case that you've taken on too much and it's time to course-correct so that you can stay the distance. Write a list of everything that needs to be done and, for each thing, consider ways to either de-prioritize or delegate it.

+ Consider any resistance you may have to 'settling down'. What are all the words and other associations you have with this concept? Do you think it sounds 'boring'? Are you afraid you'll get stuck in the mud if you don't keep moving on to the next hot thing? Or perhaps it's the opposite and you're actually craving more peace and stability? Journal about whatever feelings and thoughts come up.

QUEEN of WANDS.

QUEEN OF WANDS

You're 'on' today. You've made all your work deadlines, done all your admin and cleared out your inbox. And you even found time to join your co-workers for lunch, something that almost never happens. But something's off.

One of your colleagues remains at her desk. Funny that no one else notices.

'I'll just eat here. I'll be fine,' she says. She doesn't look fine.

'What's up?' you ask.

After several minutes of deflection, she finally tells you. There's a position open in another department. She wants to go for it, but she would be the only female candidate in what's rumoured to be a pool of aggressive men. You both know she's more than qualified for the role.

'Do you really want to go for it?' you ask.

'Yes.'

'When's the deadline for your application?'

'Tomorrow morning.'

'Find an empty meeting room while I go get us some sandwiches. I think we've got some work to do.'

The Queen of Wands is the ultimate feminine firebrand, bursting with 'can-do' energy and boldly leading the way. This card is the cheerleader of the Wands suit. It's upbeat, full of enthusiasm and can rouse a team at the drop of a hat. When the chips are down, the Queen of Wands implores you to hold your head up.

The Queen of Wands card shows a person sitting on a throne, holding a wand in one hand and a flower in the other. This card helps us find the bright side, even if there's only a tiny little sliver of light. The Queen is aware of the emotional toll making an effort can take and brings us the boost that we need. This card says, 'I know you can do it, even if you don't feel like you can.' Call on the Queen of Wands when this positive brand of 'mother energy' is needed; when you need to hear the message: 'I know it's hard. But I know you can keep going. I'll be here to help all the way.'

JOURNAL PROMPTS

+ Who are your Queen of Wands role models? Bring to mind an individual (it could be a public figure or a person in your life) who embodies the nurturing, can-do energy of this card. What advice would they give you about your current situation? What would they say to you to help coach you through this moment? Note down everything that comes up, as if you're writing in their voice.

+ Bring to mind a time when you have been the Queen of Wands for somebody else. List all the qualities you brought forth in this instance and try to feel this energy in your body. Now return to the above exercise and imagine your higher-self giving you exactly the pep talk you need to boost your confidence, help you feel held and develop your trust in your own abilities as you move forwards.

KING of WANDS

KING OF WANDS

You love taking the lead and you're thrilled to be organizing a big fundraising dinner for your University. All the major donors and esteemed alumni from the business school will be in attendance: the cream of the crop.

You want to make this a memorable occasion, so you're getting creative. As the dinner is being billed as 'world cuisine', each attendee will get a special ticket that denotes which dish they'll get.

Imagine how surprised some of the millionaires will be when they're brought a bowl of rice and nothing else. Since about ten per cent of the world's population lives in extreme poverty, you've planned for ten per cent of the attendees to be served a 'meal' that reflects this. The rest will be served a sumptuous five-course feast.

Of course, it's a risky plan, but it's one that you hope will raise awareness about those who are woefully underprivileged. Or, at the very least, make the school newspaper.

The King of Wands is just as enthusiastic as its partner card, the Queen. Like his feminine counterpart, the King sits on his throne holding a wand. He's clothed in bright robes, reflecting the fiery energy of the Wands suit. This card represents someone who is very comfortable with being centre stage, even if they have to elbow a few folks out of the way to get there.

This is a card of confidence and signals strong – perhaps sometimes even forceful – leadership. Not one to be stingy with the charm, the King is ready to smooth things over if feathers are ruffled… but will still insist that his way is the right way.

The King of Wands asks you not to take 'no' for an answer, especially if that 'no' will detract from your leadership potential. Its message is clear: 'This is not the time to sit back and let others lead. Light your torch and hold it high for others to follow.'

JOURNAL PROMPTS

+ What makes you shy away from taking the lead? Bring to mind one or more situations where you are taking a back seat (either in a work situation or in your personal life) and write down all the fears that come up when you consider pushing forwards with your agenda instead. Is it fear of being challenged? Are you afraid you may hurt others' feelings? Now create a separate list imagining the potential future outcomes of you boldly taking the reins. What do you see?

+ When you think about what makes a 'good leader', who is the first person that comes to mind? Whoever it is, list all the leadership qualities they embody that you admire. Now try to imagine them on their path to the top. What less admirable traits may they have employed to reach their position of influence? Does this make them any less worthy of your respect and veneration? When it comes to ethical use of power, where do you draw the line?

ACE of SWORDS.

ACE OF SWORDS

Making decisions is something you're not used to at all. Maybe it's been due to sheer luck, but throughout your life things have just happened. The CEO of one company heard you speak at an event and offered you a job on the spot. And you took it. The head of diversity of another company met you at a networking event. Two days later, they called with a better offer. You took that, too.

But this time it's different.

Two job offers are on the table. Both corporate jobs. Both high-paying. Both stressful.

You've followed the path laid out for you ever since you were at school. Your good grades led you to the best school in town, then the best university. It was easy – and a little boring. You didn't even have to think.

Now you do. And after thinking, analysing and ruminating, you've finally made a decision.

Which job will you take? Neither. You were never sure you wanted the corporate life anyway. Maybe it's time to decide for yourself what kind of life you want.

The Ace of Swords heralds the start of the Swords suit, which is connected to the element of Air. The suit's main themes are intellect, communication and truth-seeking and the Ace of Swords paves the way for these themes to come forth in different aspects of daily life.

This card is your travelling partner on the quest for truth. The sword on the card helps you cut through forests of confusion so you can see your way forwards. The Ace of Swords represents setting an intention to develop a clear understanding of your environment and yourself. Connect with the energy of the Ace of Swords to help you mentally prepare for a new start, or to re-evaluate a situation with fresh eyes and clarity.

JOURNAL PROMPTS

+ When was the last time you clearly defined your personal values? Take some time in the coming days to reflect on what is most important to you, taking notes as you consider this. What will you come up with? When you have a list of four to five core values, try applying them to any area of your life you have been grappling with. What's out of alignment? What choice would help you course-correct?

+ If you have a decision to make, take a moment to write out an old-fashioned list of pros and cons. Now review your list. Whose best interests are you putting first here? How might the list be altered if you were brutally honest with yourself about what is actually a 'pro' and a 'con' for *you*?

TWO OF SWORDS

You've never seen eye to eye with your sibling. Not only is there a huge age difference, but the two of you have completely different views on politics, religion, sports and every other subject known to humankind. The historic fights between the two of you have ruined many a family gathering. Most people can't believe you're in the same family, much less have the same mother.

But your mother is gone now. And it's just the two of you.

Between the time you left home, decades ago, and your mother's funeral, you may have spoken to your sibling twice a year – usually when you call each other on your birthdays, just to be polite. The physical distance brought relief. Be honest: they don't even cross your mind anymore, do they?

You've blocked them out. And no matter what anyone thinks or says, you can't take the risk of establishing open communication again. You've refused all contact.

But time brings healing. And it gives you space to think. And wonder. What would happen if you picked up the phone and just called to say hi?

The Two of Swords signals rigidity and blockage. Nothing gets in, nothing goes out. A tight-jawed refusal is connected to this card, which is often depicted as someone holding two crossed swords at their chest. The Two of Swords reflects someone who has closed themselves off entirely, refusing to give in or change their thoughts, even when under pressure to reconsider. Depending on the situation, this could be positive or negative.

Use the Two of Swords as a psychic mirror to see what has prompted the block. Is your intuition telling you to protect yourself, your thoughts and what you know in your soul to be true? The energy of this card can help you stand in your power. However, if the voice in your head whispers a message of reconciliation, consider taking that advice.

JOURNAL PROMPTS

+ What about your current situation could benefit from you putting a firm boundary in place? Use your intuition to 'feel into' any area that feels energetically 'leaky', or as if you are taking on too much of another person's (or society's) 'stuff'. Creating this boundary might mean saying 'no', or it could mean extracting yourself from a situation that is not serving you. Practise writing out a script for how you might go about this.

+ Bring to mind a person, a situation or a discussion you have decided point-blank that you want nothing to do with. List all your reasons for this: perhaps you have been burned in the past, or maybe popular opinion says you 'shouldn't' get involved. Try to dig deep and get personal with your reasons. How much of your reticence is fear-based? And what exactly are you afraid of?

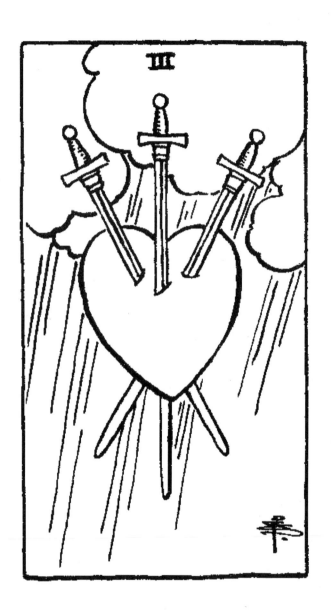

THREE OF SWORDS

Yet another meeting is taking place without you, even though you're part of the project team. It's the second time this has happened this month.

You didn't think anything of it the first time. Perhaps your boss's assistant had forgotten to include you. But this time, when you asked your line manager about it, she said, 'I'll let you know when we need you'.

During your last performance review, your manager was polite, but distracted. She didn't seem interested in any of your accomplishments that year. You sensed something was off, but you weren't sure what.

The situation has really begun to bother you. You love your job. It was an absolute dream when you started. But when the company was sold to a large international conglomerate, things changed. You were left out of more and more, not given approval to attend conferences and you're beginning to feel ignored – except by one department.

An invitation from HR has just landed in your inbox for a meeting on Friday at 4.45pm.

The Three of Swords shows three weapons piercing a heart, representing a painful revelation. A secret has been laid bare; the truth is out in the open. Yes, it hurts, perhaps more than you think you can handle. But at least whatever you suspected was going on behind the scenes has been revealed.

This card acknowledges your pain. It asks you to feel your way through it, with the reminder that this is how you get to the other side. The Three of Swords tells us that, sometimes, we hold on to the pain of a situation because that's the only thing left. It tells us that at least 'something' is there. But that 'something' needs to be released. The Three of Swords asks you to love your pain enough to give it a merciful death, so that you can move on.

JOURNAL PROMPTS

+ Without overthinking it, free-write about a painful situation from your past that you still feel is affecting you. Perhaps you feel it has done lasting damage to your self-esteem, or permanently altered your worldview, leading you to always expect the worst. Let whatever lasting feelings you have about it spill over onto the page. When you're done, send unconditional love to the part of you that is holding on to the hurt. Then burn or flush the page.

+ If you are feeling fearful about how a certain situation may play out, write out a list of possible 'worst-case scenarios'. What past situations are feeding these fears? Then, for each one, write about how you would deal with it should it happen. While the future is still unknown, what can you begin to put in place now as a buffer against life's inevitable twists and turns?

FOUR OF SWORDS

'What the hell are you doing?!'

You normally don't scream at the kids. Not like that, with that shrill pitch to your voice and a crazed look in your eyes. But your youngest apparently didn't want breakfast this morning, so they threw it on the floor.

Now the cereal is everywhere and so is your mind.

You're on edge. And you've screamed at them — just for being a child.

It's 7am, but you've been awake since 4am because of cramps. All you want is to get the kids off to school so you can go to work. The restaurant will probably be packed today.

But if you snapped at your child for throwing cereal on the floor, how will you react at work if someone complains about their order?

In fact, when was the last time you had a day off? Yes, your team members need you at the restaurant, but they also need you to be healthy and in control.

The Four of Swords is the card of self-care and it brings the message to lay your weapons down and allow your soul to sink into a deep, much-needed rest. The card sometimes depicts a figure in repose. Three swords hang on the wall over them, while one lies beneath them. The Four of Swords signals that it's time to give your body a chance to heal, physically or mentally – and you need to do it *now*.

Call on the Four of Swords when you need to face up to the myriad excuses you've made to yourself in order to avoid taking a break. It also forces us to take a good look at the repercussions of burning out, such as moodiness, depression and an inability to get things done. The Four of Swords serves as a warning to look out for your wellbeing. Tending to your own self-care first and foremost is the right thing for you and for those around you.

JOURNAL PROMPTS

+ What does 'self-care' mean to you? List all the activities and practices – physical, mental, emotional and spiritual – that help you replenish your reserves of energy, creativity and compassion. Choose three things from your list that you can give yourself this week and physically make space for them in your calendar.

+ What are all the excuses you make to prevent yourself from taking a break? Write down as many as you can think of: perhaps you think it's 'lazy', perhaps there isn't time, or perhaps you feel that you'll be letting others down. For each one, writing in the voice of a loving parent or mentor figure, come up with a counter-argument that shows how taking a time-out will actually serve you and others.

FIVE OF SWORDS

The conflict over whether your daughter can join the boys' football team has taken an awful turn.

It all started innocently enough. Girls' football teams were the norm where you used to live and your child was the star of her school's team. Moving to a new town had taken a toll on your family. Getting her back into sports could be a much-needed step towards normality.

But her new school doesn't have a girls' football team. Only a boys' team.

There is no question of her joining it, the coach says. 'We don't do that type of thing here.'

That's when the fighting started. And the protests. And then the threats.

After a long talk between you and your daughter you make a difficult decision: you accept that she won't be able to play.

A cloud hovers over your family for a week – but then you find something as you unpack the last of the removal boxes.

Your old baseball bat. And it's just the right weight for your daughter to hold.

The Five of Swords traditionally represents some type of loss after a conflict. The card often depicts an armed 'victor' watching as their opponents, who've abandoned their weapons, walk away from the battleground. But this is only the superficial meaning. After all, the definition of 'loss' depends on the context; walking away from a stressful situation can actually be a win.

The Five of Swords asks you to weigh the worth of the fight against your wellbeing. If winning at all costs is your goal, by all means go ahead. But when you're ready to give up the fight on your own terms, the Five of Swords can be your talisman for turning what might seem from the outside like a no-win situation into something that actually works in your favour.

JOURNAL PROMPTS

+ What past perceived 'loss' actually turned out to be a win for you? Perhaps it was a painful break-up that ended up paving the way for you to meet the love of your life. Maybe you were unfairly fired from a job you were only doing for the money, spurring you to pursue a passion project that you find far more satisfying. With these reflections in mind, consider what about your current situation could contain a hidden 'win' that you can't see just yet.

+ Could your pride or your attachment to being perceived in a certain way be preventing you from letting go of something that is actually holding you back? In the voice of your future-self, write a letter to the 'you' who is afraid of losing face or who feels they 'need' to win on principle. What can this future-self see about your current situation?

SIX OF SWORDS

Your neighbourhood is your lifeblood. The people, the spirit of community and the history are all part of your DNA – or, at least, they were. The neighbourhood is changing.

It's losing its soul to gentrification. Gone is the local grocers, one of the few places in walking distance where you could get fresh fruits and vegetables. In its place is an extremely hip and expensive coffee shop. The people who lived there when you were growing up, mostly low-to-middle income folks who worked hard for what they had, have moved away or died. Their once-affordable flats have been transformed into living spaces pulled straight from magazine spreads or styled social media posts.

You returned to your childhood home after your parents passed away because you wanted to bring back what you've learned during your travels and use it to help your neighbours, but the neighbours you once knew are gone – and no one wants your help.

Perhaps it's time to move on.

The Six of Swords reflects a slow, steady move away from someone or something – if not physically, then mentally. The card often shows three figures in a boat sailing away with a cargo of six swords. The decision to leave was probably difficult, but it was necessary. Times have changed and the world has moved on. The Six of Swords gives permission to disconnect from what is no longer in alignment and to move towards the new. There's no anger in the decision, just a sense of resignation and even peace.

The Six of Swords is helpful for working through mental transitions and shifts in thinking. It signals the thought processes we go through when faced with those 'should I stay or should I go?' situations. Meditate on the Six of Swords to remain faithful to your decision to move on in your life. Even if you're not sure where you're going, when you get there, you'll realize it's where you should be.

JOURNAL PROMPTS

+ What are you clinging on to that is no longer relevant or appropriate in your current situation? Write down the first thing that comes up when you consider this question. It could be a physical thing, or it could be a belief or a way of doing things. Instead of continuing to try and 'make it work', what comes up for you when you consider simply putting it down and moving on? Journal about any feelings that are present or ideas that arise to fill the space this creates.

+ Bring to mind an image of yourself ten years ago. What were your chief concerns at this time in your life? What brought you joy and what created stress? And what do you know now, about yourself and about life in general, that you have learned in the years since? Write down any observations that come up. How could you benefit from this 'long-view' perspective in your current situation?

SEVEN OF SWORDS

Your son is smart, attractive – and irresponsible. And it's your fault. Or at least, that's what you believe.

As a single parent, you made sure he had the best of everything in an effort to make up for the fact that you weren't bringing him up in a two-parent household. For example, during his teens, he had his own bank account, which you put money into. All he had to do in return was study and get good grades so he could get into university.

And he did, taking with him all the things he learned from you. But one thing he didn't learn was responsibility. The last two semesters have been a shit show: his grades are poor, money runs through his fingers and he refuses to get a part-time job to help cover his tuition.

Did you coddle him too much? Should you cut him off financially so he's forced to take care of himself? Whatever you decide, you know he'll accuse you of being an awful parent. Again.

But something has to change.

The traditional meaning of the Seven of Swords is dishonesty. The card usually shows somebody looking over their shoulder, running from the scene with their arms full of swords. The implication is that the person has shirked their duties or turned their back on an issue that should be dealt with. But there's an additional, perhaps more modern, meaning to this card: guilt.

The Seven of Swords asks you to examine your actions carefully. Are you fuelled by a sense of obligation? Are you taking responsibility for something (or someone) when that's not your role? Are you afraid of making a decision for fear of getting it wrong?

Perhaps there's a need to work through some lingering sensations of regret or remorse, especially if you've been mentally punishing yourself over a misstep. Use the energy of the Seven of Swords to identify these feelings so you can address them, take whatever action seems to be in alignment with *your* truth and then move on.

JOURNAL PROMPTS

+ Is it really possible to always 'do the right thing'? Can you think of anybody, either in your own life or in the public eye, who has *never* made a mistake? With your responses to these questions in mind, write down all the standards you are holding yourself to when it comes to your current situation. Are the expectations you have placed on yourself realistic? What might you learn if you allowed yourself to make a misstep?

+ Are there areas of your life in which are you taking responsibility for another person's actions or feelings? With one of these situations in mind, write down all the things you stand to gain from shouldering this burden. Does it mean that the other person will like you? That they won't have to suffer? That you won't have to be 'the bad guy'? Now consider what it is you think that they can't 'handle' about the situation. Is it really helping them for you to carry it all?

EIGHT OF SWORDS

You've stayed too long in this relationship. Far too long. But if you left, where would you go? What would you do? How would you take care of yourself financially?

These questions have been hounding you for years, as things have got progressively worse. And they've locked you in place. You have no choice; you have to stay. This is the only path you can coo.

What you may be missing – or, let's be truthful, ignoring – are the multiple texts and phone calls you're receiving. Your friends and family are pleading with you to leave.

They don't understand. They have no idea that you're worried about the basics: food and shelter.

But are you sure about that? If that's the case, why is your best friend on the phone, right now, with yet another offer to stay at their place. You wouldn't have to worry about anything. Your only task would be to heal.

All you have to do is reach out and accept the help.

The Eight of Swords reflects a feeling of being trapped, of believing that there's no way out. A sense of helplessness permeates this card. In some decks, the card shows a person, blindfolded and bound, surrounded by swords. But the card can also remind us that we can find a way to free ourselves.

This card asks you to realize that you have options and that you have the power to free yourself. Do you feel stuck in a situation and can't see a path out? Are obligations closing in on you? The Eight of Swords suggests that help is close at hand – perhaps closer than you think. If you look around, there may be a way out of your situation at your fingertips. You just have to remove your mental blindfold and look.

JOURNAL PROMPTS

+ Who in your network can you call on to help you out with whatever situation is currently making you feel trapped? Maybe you feel trapped in your job, or you're faced with a conundrum you just can't seem to find a resolution to. With this situation in mind, scroll through the contacts in your phone, or look through your friends on social media, and see whose name jumps out. It may not be somebody you would usually think to call on for help, but why not give it a shot?

+ Do you have a tendency to do everything yourself, believing it will be the quickest and most effective way to get things done? And do you then end up exhausted and burned out? Write down everything you are currently juggling, including tasks related to both your work and home life. For each thing you write down, consider whether you could delegate all or part of the task to somebody else. In some cases this may not be the best solution, or even possible, but notice how it feels to at least consider lightening your load.

NINE OF SWORDS

'Follow your dream,' you said to yourself.

'Live your truth,' you said to yourself.

But in the excitement of landing your dream position at an art gallery and resigning from your corporate gig, you didn't consider the pay cut. Or the loss of the bonus. Or that your rent would go up.

You're calculating your budget and you're worried. For years, you took the financial security that came with your old job, and the lifestyle it gave you, for granted. How will you pay your bills now? Did you make the right move?

What in the world have you done?

All these questions are swimming in your head, for now. But these questions have answers and you will find them. Soon, you'll take action: you'll get your spending under control, you'll find a cheaper place to live and you'll wake up every day grateful for the fact you're no longer caught up in the corporate grind.

But right now, the only thing you can do is worry.

The Nine of Swords is the 'dark night of the soul' card. It represents deep, intense worry: the type of worry that keeps you up at night and wears you out during the day. Themes connected to this card include anxiety and stress, and it can also signal feeling overwhelmed with day-to-day issues and an inability to see the light at the end of the tunnel.

This card prompts you to look at your daily challenges. Are they piling up into one uncontrollable mess? If so, the Nine of Swords asks you to take a look at the 'why' behind the mess. When you do that, you'll be able to see your patterns – the behaviours that led you here – and hopefully begin to plan a way out. And when this part of your life is behind you, you may well ask yourself what that worrying was for.

JOURNAL PROMPTS

+ Bring to mind a time when you felt completely overwhelmed, to the point that you were unable to think straight. Perhaps you feel this way about a part of your life right now. Write down everything about the situation: the practical details, as well as the feelings, fears and insecurities attached to it. When everything is on the page, read back over what you've read as if you are your own analyst or therapist. What pattern emerges? What is at the root of your fears?

+ Think about somebody who has faced terrible adversity and come out the other side stronger and wiser than ever before. This could be somebody in your life, or somebody in the public eye. What helped them to overcome their challenges? What do you think they learned about themselves and the world in the process? Journal about what comes up.

TEN OF SWORDS

The five of you formed an a cappella group at university. At first it was just for fun. You performed at campus parties and in local jazz clubs. As a group, you were tight – both in sound and friendship. The camaraderie was clear on stage. People took notice, especially the big producer that happened to be passing through town.

The next few years were a whirlwind. First came the contract, then the album. There was even buzz around possible awards. But as the accolades and money came in, you realized, as a group, that the love of singing had left you. Now, performing has become tedious. The spark and camaraderie are gone. No matter how much you all try, you just can't get it back. Your fans have begun to notice.

It just isn't fun anymore.

The farewell tour will be short and you will stick to small venues, catering to the fans who were with you in the beginning. It's the right thing to do for a group that has run its course.

The Ten of Swords represents an ending. You've tried everything to keep a situation going, but each new innovation or idea has failed. It's over. There can also be an element of self-pity and a tendency to wallow in feelings of guilt with the Ten of Swords. But if there's one positive thing about this card, it's this: things have got as bad as they're going to get. They can't get any worse. You can't go any lower. You have reached the end of the line.

Are you hanging on to a cause or idea in the hope that everything will somehow get better? Are you awaiting a positive outcome you know in your heart will never come? Or do you just need your mind to catch up with the answer your subconscious already knows? If you're looking for a definite sign that shouts 'it's over' (or even 'get over yourself') the Ten of Swords is your card.

JOURNAL PROMPTS

+ Something in your life has run its course. It could be a job, a relationship, a passion project or even a way of being. Whatever it is, take some time to write a farewell letter to this part of your life. Go into detail about all the good times you had. Note when things started to wane. Give thanks for what you learned along the way and explain why you're ready to move on. When you're done, either burn the letter or bury it.

+ List all the things in your life that didn't turn out the way you'd hoped. All the 'failures', the missed opportunities and the dreams that didn't come true. For each one, imagine that you had got what you wanted and think of one positive outcome and one negative outcome from this imagined situation. Notice how for everything you 'missed out on', you also dodged a potential bullet.

PAGE of SWORDS.

PAGE OF SWORDS

You honestly didn't mean to piss off your neighbourhood's newly formed 'Protect Our Planet' (POP) group – you had no idea you were breaking the recycling regulations. Who the heck would know that cardboard is supposed to go in the green container, bottles in the brown container and milk cartons in a special biodegradable plastic bag that is supposed to be hung from a hook on the side of the damned brown container?

The POP bunch is an unruly crowd, though. They take no excuses, especially with our planet in such peril. Pollution, greenhouse gases and neighbours who can't honour the local recycling rules are all equal threats to the environment in their eyes.

As the group stands at your door, the leader steps forwards and shows you the evidence of your crime in a video captured on their phone. Then they announce your penalty: one bar of vegan chocolate for each POP member, a donation and a pinky promise to never break the rules again.

For a group of ten-year-olds, they are pretty ruthless.

The Page of Swords, like all pages in the tarot, represents youth or a youthful approach to using the intellectual energy of their suit. The Page believes in reason and integrity, using the sword of truth to slash away confusion or unethical behaviour. To the Page, right and wrong are clear cut, with no ambiguity.

This card can be helpful when fresh eyes are needed to see what's real, and to see to the heart of the issues being faced. The energy of the Page of Swords can help you analyse a problem and move directly to a clear-cut solution. This card asks you to be open to discovery and learning. Use it to help you take a few steps back from a situation so you can see the big picture through non-jaded eyes.

JOURNAL PROMPTS

+ What would ten-year-old you do in your current situation? Take a step back and imagine the solutions a younger and less world-weary version of yourself might come up with. Imagine you still believe that the 'good guys' always win in the end and write down several potential outcomes to any challenges you are facing with this idea in mind. What steps would you take today if you knew this outcome was possible?

+ Bring to mind a moral dilemma you are currently facing or have faced in the past. What is the truly ethical thing to do? Now consider each of the key players in the situation. For each person or group involved, consider what is their truth and list all the different reasons for this. Now do the same for yourself. Notice anywhere you have been serving your own needs at the expense of others. How can you close up the gap in values?

KNIGHT *of* SWORDS .

KNIGHT OF SWORDS

'I know I'm right,' the new boss says.

'How do you know?' you reply.

'Because I saw him stuff something into his pocket!'

You've been a security guard at this shop for a few years, but your new boss, a retired police officer, has more work experience. They know shoplifters. But you also feel sure that your boss is profiling the young man you're both looking at.

'Are you sure it's the right guy? The one I saw on the monitor looked taller,' you say.

'Look, kid. I've been at this a lot longer than you. And there's clearly something in his back pocket. Now, you take notes while I confront the suspect,' your boss replies.

But you know that this kid hasn't stolen anything. He's been coming to the shop since he was a child. You want your new boss to see that not everyone fits their 'profile' of a shoplifter. You calmly approach the young man. 'Hey bro,' you say. 'Could you show me what's in your back pocket?'

'Sure!' He reaches into his back pocket. He pulls out a battered old notebook. The pages are filled with his poetry.

The Knight of Swords represents keen, steely intellect and signals someone with confidence and authority. They are committed to finding the truth – by any means necessary. The Knight of Swords believes in speaking their mind and getting straight to the point. May the universe help anyone who gets between this knight and the truth. As with almost all court cards, the qualities of the Knight of Swords can be positive or negative, depending on the situation.

Do you sometimes wobble when you're trying to exude authority or take a stand? The energy of the Knight of Swords can help you balance yourself with its get-to-the-point qualities. Does your unwillingness to 'take a side' sometimes lead to confusion or indecisiveness? This card can help you make a decision with confidence. One important thing to remember about the Knight of Swords, though: too much of this card's energy can be overbearing, insensitive or block-headed.

JOURNAL PROMPTS

+ Who models decisive leadership for you? In situations where a clear path forwards is needed, it's a gift to be able to set a course and stick to it, regardless of what others may have to say about it. Come up with some examples of individuals – either from your own life or in the public realm – who embody positive and powerful leadership qualities. What can you learn from them about standing your own ground?

+ Imagine your current situation is part of the plot in a TV detective story. What 'truth' needs to be unveiled before everything can be resolved? If you are the detective, what question should you be asking to help you get to the bottom of things? List these lines of enquiry and, for each one, consider how you might gather the information you need. Who are the 'suspects' and what might they be hiding?

QUEEN of SWORDS.

QUEEN OF SWORDS

You've never really taken a liking to the term #girlboss, but apparently that's how the people working under you refer to you. You've gained a reputation for your clear communication, coupled with a caring but no-nonsense approach.

So when the Managing Director comes to your office and asks if you have time to talk, you are happy to agree. But his next question surprises you.

'How am I doing as your manager?' he asks. 'And I want you to be honest, as always.'

You aren't sure if this is a test, but screw it. You decide to tell the truth. 'Well, I see someone who has given their all to this company, stuck with it through all of its ups and downs and who is trying their best to keep it together. I see someone who loves their job, but is tired,' you say.

'Thank you for saying that. You were the one person I knew would say what all the others were thinking. Which is why you're the first to know: I'm retiring. And I'm recommending you as my successor.'

The Queen of Swords signals somebody with a loving, honest, feminine energy. They're not one for mind games or skirting the truth and will also wait for the appropriate moment to have a difficult conversation. The Queen of Swords represents frankness, candour and a willingness to clear the air, with everybody's best interests in mind.

Meditate on this card when you need a gentle nudge to get to the point. The Queen of Swords is the mother figure that tells it like it is in order to redirect your focus and send you off in the right direction. Do you need more honesty from others around you – and yourself? This Queen's energy can create a soothing, safe space in which the truth can come out.

JOURNAL PROMPTS

+ Bring to mind a situation where you have been avoiding telling the whole truth, whether from a fear of hurt feelings, pushback or potentially offending somebody. What feeling does this blockage create in your mind and/or body? How might it be impeding forward motion in a project or relationship? Write down the truth, the whole truth and nothing but the truth. How can you go about creating the right conditions in order for the truth to come forth?

+ How does it make you feel when somebody else is brutally honest with you? Write down the different feelings that come up. Now put yourself in the shoes of the person doing the truth-telling. What is their intention? With these reflections in mind, journal about why you think so many of us avoid telling the truth, and what could be achieved if we were less afraid of hearing it.

KING of SWORDS.

KING OF SWORDS

You've just lost the election by the slimmest of margins. Some of your constituents are begging you to fight, to call for a recount. But it's been a bruising campaign, with your opponent pulling out all the stops to make sure every piece of misinformation possible was out there, casting you in the most negative light they could.

It was tempting to go low and you came close to losing your patience, but in the end you refused. Even when your opponent questioned your intelligence and integrity, you stuck to your message and hoped that voters could cut through the noise. Some of them did, most didn't.

But there was something beyond the election that you wanted people to see. And that was how you operated. How you carried yourself with dignity and stood by your truth. You were fair and just.

Was this enough to win you the election? No. But it is enough to leave you with a long list of people who have already signed up for your next campaign, eager to work for you when you decide to run for office in the future.

The King of Swords is the epitome of integrity and logic. He applies his high standards to both himself and those around him and is fair and impartial. The only side he takes is the one of 'right'. The King of Swords solves problems and enacts justice in a swift and decisive manner. It's always business, never personal with this card.

Meditate on this card as motivation for leading with integrity and having the courage of your convictions. The King of Swords can help you root yourself in the truth, even when everyone and everything else wavers. Do you need to rise above back-stabbing and in-fighting? The King can help you do so with authority. And while your actions may not always be popular, you can be sure you are on the side of good.

JOURNAL PROMPTS

+ What's more important: personality or character? One speaks to the 'public' face we show and the behaviours we enact to get people to like us; the other speaks to our inner moral code. Consider some areas in your life where you have been letting personality override character. What actions can you take in public that would be more aligned with the person you are on the inside?

+ Zoom out and survey the different situations currently playing out in your life. Where can you spot incidents of injustice – both big and small? Write them down and, for each one of these glitches in the moral fabric of life, think about what you can do to help ensure that justice prevails. This might mean getting more politically active; it might mean reaching out to let somebody know you're on their side; or it may mean setting a boundary around a personal truth.

ACE ♣ CUPS.

ACE OF CUPS

You held on to your fur baby for as long as you could, physically and mentally. But she was so sick. The vet had warned you that the time would come. 'She'll tell you when she's ready to go,' they said. And she did.

Each morning when you hugged her and snuggled your nose in her fur, you could feel her becoming weaker and fading away. Then, one day, she couldn't get up for her walk. Her eyes met yours. 'It's time,' they said.

You made the appointment with the vet and you let her go. But she wasn't just a pet. She was a friend who had been with you for ten years, through thick and thin.

That was a year ago. You promised yourself that you would never, ever have another pet again. The heartbreak of losing your best friend was too great. But on your way home from work, you pass by a pet adoption fair. You shouldn't, but you do. And that's where you see her: this tiny, scrappy little thing fighting her way to the front of the cage to get a look at you.

Maybe, just maybe, you can open your heart again.

The Cups take us on a journey through the element of Water, and the Ace of Cups is where we begin. The card usually shows a hand holding a cup or chalice overflowing with water. It says that emotions, and the desires attached to them, cannot be ignored. This card prepares us to open up and dive deep into our feelings.

Visualize the Ace of Cups as the guide of your emotions: walking before you as you begin (or continue) your journey towards the inner sanctum of your heart. This card can help you connect to your feelings in a safe and nurturing way, and it can also signal new beginnings for connections and relationships. Meditate on the Ace of Cups to open you up to the many possibilities of love.

JOURNAL PROMPTS

+ Who or what in your world is asking for your love? It could be a person, or perhaps a cause, an idea or a passion project. Whatever comes up, consider why you may have been shy about giving it the full force of your loving attention. Is it that you don't have the time for it? Or that you're afraid of getting hurt? Now write down a few of the potential positive outcomes you might see if you opened your heart and went all in.

+ If you are looking for romantic love, meditate on this card to help you get clarity on exactly what you desire in a partnership. List all the qualities that you value in a partner and, for each one, write down why this is important to you at this juncture in your life. When you're done, review the list and try to conjure how it feels to be around this person. Keep 'them' with you as you go about your day.

TWO OF CUPS

Moving to another city where you don't have any contacts is hard enough. Moving to another country where you don't know anybody is an entirely different matter. But you've done it. After successfully negotiating a job rotation, your employer armed you with 50 hours of language courses, an outdated brochure of cultural events and a plane ticket.

Your one big mistake: thinking not only that your new co-workers would help you, but that they *should* help you. They should be honoured to have a high-flyer from headquarters on their team. Right? Wrong. And in a big way.

Three weeks have passed and you're struggling to fit in. You're sitting in the office alone, as everyone else has gone out for drinks. Except for one person: the office assistant. Yes, they've been side-eyeing you for weeks and you're sure you've heard a couple of exasperated sighs in reaction to your cultural screw-ups. But at least they acknowledge your existence.

Go ahead. Walk over and say 'Hi'. You may even make a new friend in the process.

The Two of Cups represents the spirit of partnership and consensus. The card often shows two figures facing each other while holding cups. A connection has been established. There's a slight distance between them, a space in which possibilities can grow and flourish. The Two of Cups honours positive expectations and celebrates the potential for collaboration. If there has been strife in the air, this card signals the chance for a truce.

Use the energy of the Two of Cups to establish – or to re-establish – a connection. Perhaps you're seeking out a like-minded person for collaboration, whether that's in the boardroom or between the sheets. The Two of Cups signals a willingness to take on a partner and a willingness to be a better partner yourself.

JOURNAL PROMPTS

+ Where in your current situation are you insisting on going it alone, when in fact it could be beneficial to seek another pair of hands to share the load? It can often feel simpler to attempt to get things done solo, with nobody else's feelings or ways of doing things to consider. But how might this attitude be holding you back? Review your to-do list and choose one thing you can ask for help with, even if it's just as an experiment.

+ How could you be a better partner or collaborator? This often comes down to listening and actually taking the time to hear another person's needs or ideas. Think about the people in your life who have done this for you in the past and write down a few ways in which you felt supported by them. Now consider who in your life you could offer this same support to.

THREE OF CUPS

Apparently, you were supposed to bring the mead.

You facepalm yourself and laugh. 'Oh my gosh, everyone, I'm sorry. I must have missed that text.'

Actually, you didn't miss it. You just had no clue what 'mead' was and were too embarrassed to ask.

'Now, about that ritual – who'll cast the circle and call the quarters?' says one of your friends.

'Wait. Who'll do the *what?*' another friend asks. 'How can you "call the quarters" in a circle? Shouldn't that be… '

'Oh, stop over-analysing! We're supposed to be setting intentions for the new moon,' you hiss playfully. But first, you have to find the instructions, which are in the bottom of your backpack. As you burrow into your bag, you start giggling.

Then one coven mate joins you. Then the other. Until the three of you are laughing at yourselves, celebrating the wonderful mess you've made of your first New Moon ritual.

'Can we just skip ahead to cakes and mead?' one asks.

'We don't have cakes, but we have doughnuts. And as for mead,' you say, laughing, 'we've got ginger ale.'

The Three of Cups is the card of pure, unadulterated, communal joy. This is the card of celebration: it signals marking a special event or achievement, or simply celebrating being with your loved ones. Traditionally, the card depicts three people raising their cups in a happy toast.

Meditate on the Three of Cups to help you celebrate your wins as a team, both big and small. The card also asks you to celebrate yourself; modesty has no place here. Does giving yourself a great big pat on the back make you uncomfortable? The Three of Cups suggests at least trying it. And, if you have trouble, allow your friends to heap praise and adoration on the wonderful being that you are.

JOURNAL PROMPTS

+ If you had to choose one thing to celebrate today, what would it be? And who would you call to celebrate with you? You don't have to wait for your birthday, for a success at work or even until the next New Moon to get together and celebrate *life*. If you can't meet in person, organize a group call or digital get-together with your friends and each spend a few minutes sharing what you want to celebrate about the others.

+ Go through the contacts list in your phone and, for each name that 'pops', send them a text telling them something you love and appreciate about them. Hopefully they'll respond in kind and, by the end of the day, you'll have a treasure trove of loving messages in your inbox that you can look to any time you're feeling blue.

FOUR OF CUPS

You have absolutely no chance of finding a partner. You know it. And you're going to make damn sure your friends know it over dinner.

'Look at this idiot', you snarl, as you swipe and pass your phone to your buddies, making sure even your friend's guest, who you've never met before, gets a good look at the screen.

You rage on. After some throat-clearing, the friend who brought a guest along tries to change the subject. But you miss their signal as you continue to swipe, detailing the shortcomings of each prospect.

You also fail to notice that your friend's attractive plus-one has been attempting to start a conversation with you for the last half hour. Eventually, they lean over to your friend to whisper something, then they get up and leave.

'Oh, who was that?' you ask your friend.

'Someone I thought would be a good match for you. But they had to leave.'

'Oh! Well, why didn't you introduce me?'

'I never got the chance.'

The Four of Cups reflects the opportunities for happiness and fulfilment that surround you, if only you'd take a look. The card sometimes shows a person sitting on the ground, looking downcast. A hand holding a cup floats next to them, unnoticed. Three more cups are on the ground.

This card can represent the full range of self-reflection, from a desire to go within to find meaning, to full-blown navel-gazing. The Four of Cups makes space for you to do your internal work – just make sure that this doesn't become self-obsession, which can block out your chances for external connection. Meditate on this card to help you reflect, carve out a space for solitude and find inner peace. And then, from this space, look up and see what the universe has to offer.

JOURNAL PROMPTS

- Over the coming days, take note whenever you find yourself getting caught up in your own thoughts. Each time you notice yourself starting to obsess over a situation where either you or the other person said or did something that's niggling at you, instead of ruminating on it, ask yourself why it's bothering you. What does it show you about yourself that you would like to improve on? What and who could you be directing your attention towards instead?

- What have you become so fixated on that you can't see the wood for the trees? Perhaps you're determined to stick to a tried-and-tested way of doing things, even though it's not bringing the results you want. Or maybe you're only interested in dating people within a certain age bracket, which cancels out half the people on your favourite dating app. With these reflections in mind, write out a series of statements beginning: 'I am ready to…', letting the universe know you're willing to change things up.

FIVE OF CUPS

Should you laugh? Cry? Feel relieved? You're not sure.

You're going into voluntary foreclosure because you couldn't keep up with your mortgage payments.

You were fine during the formalities with the bank. But now that the day has come to actually turn over the keys, the memories are all flooding back: how proud you were when you moved in; how your heart swelled when your daughter picked out her room; the day you hung your parents' wedding photo over the fireplace. All those moments are now packed away, along with everything else.

You head up to your daughter's room to check on her. 'Honey, are you okay?' you ask.

'Yeah. I'm okay,' she says sadly. 'But where will we go?'

You've been too embarrassed to tell her until now, but better late than never. 'We're going to Grandma's,' you say.

'*Really*?!' she screams with delight. Yay!'

Her excitement takes you aback.

You realize that, even though you've just lost a house, you and your daughter are potentially gaining a home.

THE NUMINOUS TAROT GUIDE

The main themes of the Five of Cups are grief, loss and overwhelming sadness. The card sometimes shows a figure draped in a dark robe with their head bowed. Three cups are overturned in front of the figure; behind them are two more cups, which are upright. The pain reflected in this card is temporary, but it hurts just the same.

The Five of Cups asks you to honour your pain and feelings of loss. It confirms that they are real and valid and that you have the right to scream, cry and do anything else necessary to acknowledge and process what you're feeling. But it also asks you to do one other thing: turn around and examine what remains.

JOURNAL PROMPTS

+ Life is a series of endings and beginnings, and while we're conditioned to celebrate new starts, we often gloss over the part where we grieve our losses. Bring to mind something that had to 'die' in order for you to be embarking on this latest phase of your life. Maybe it's a relationship, a belief or an older version of yourself. Write a goodbye letter to whatever it is, allowing yourself to feel any sadness that arises while fully acknowledging its passing.

+ At what age did you learn to squash down feelings of sadness and loss? Were you told to 'keep your chin up' and not be such a cry baby? Maybe a specific incident comes to mind, or maybe you will just get a general sense of how old you were. Now, in the voice of a loving fairy godparent, write this younger version of yourself a permission slip to express these tender feelings. Keep the piece of paper somewhere safe.

SIX OF CUPS

No one needs this many suits. You have over 20, all of them in various shades of dark blue and pretty expensive, too.

They made you feel boardroom-ready whenever you wore them. The problem is, you haven't been in a boardroom since you retired five years ago. They've been hanging in your closet ever since, taking up space and serving as a reminder that you also used to be 10 pounds lighter. Not that that's a problem.

The point is, you don't need suits now and you never will again. So what to do? After a few minutes, you have an idea.

There are three young women living in your building who are in their final year at university. They'll be looking for jobs next year and they'll need to look put together.

After having the suits professionally cleaned and boxed, you leave five of them outside the door of each student. The only thing you leave with them is a card: 'I was you 40 years ago. Wear this suit with pride. And kick some ass.' You don't leave your name. There's no need for a thank you.

The Six of Cups represents unconditional kindness and speaks to the spirit of giving without expecting anything in return: being nice just to be nice. It reflects a willingness to share what you have with the best of intentions. This card often shows two young people, surrounded by five cups. One of the figures is offering a sixth cup to the other. This card can also signal relationships with children and childhood memories.

The Six of Cups asks you to summon the energy of generosity and tenderness. Working with this card can help you find ways to be good with your thoughts, your words and your actions. It can help you to find the best in yourself and to help your fellow human beings. This is the card of pure altruism: doing things because they're the right thing to do, even when no one's watching.

JOURNAL PROMPTS

+ When was the last time somebody went out of their way to help you? How did it make you feel? And what do you think it 'cost' them? With these reflections in mind, consider ways in which you could pay it forward by offering somebody else your unconditional kindness in the coming days. What would this cost you – and what would you stand to gain? Journal about whatever comes up.

· What does 'kindness' mean to you? List everything that comes to mind as you consider this question. Your list might include certain personality traits, actions, ways of relating to others and even thoughts and ideas about how we live. Include details of specific incidents when you or somebody you know expressed kindness. How does making this list make you feel?

SEVEN OF CUPS

You've come up with a sure-fire way of making money, being your own boss and showing all the naysayers that you're a creative genius. It'll take a lot of work and some long hours, but you're a champion multitasker. Or so you'd like to believe.

Here's how it'll go. First, you'll start your handcrafted artisan soap company. Your initial offerings will be five types of soap, catering for three different skin types (you want your customers to have options). You'll then expand into body oil.

After that, you'll take your profits and pour them into an organic juice bar. The profits from *that* venture will flow into the dance studio you're setting up in the building next to the juice bar. By day, you'll offer yoga; by night, hip-hop dance classes. The money from the studio will flow into that vegan hot dog truck you've been thinking about.

All your ideas sound fabulous, but here's another: how about just doing one thing and doing it really well?

The Seven of Cups represents choices. Too many of them. The traditional imagery of this card shows a person standing in front of seven cups, with a 'surprise' popping out of each one. The selection looks pretty good, but there's something hazy and superficial about each offering, as if they haven't been fully thought through. There's potential here, but it's lacking focus.

'Focus' is the message of the Seven of Cups. Which of the many options in front of you is grounded in reality and which is no more than a foggy pipe dream? This card asks you to slow down and think. It wants you to examine your options and make a choice based on facts, not fantasy. And if you're having a difficult time making a choice, ask yourself why.

JOURNAL PROMPTS

+ Write down all of the options and choices you are currently faced with. Mentally scan each area of your life and include all the different pathways and possibilities ahead of you when it comes to work, creative projects, family, relationships and your personal development. Is the list getting long? That's a lot of scattered mental energy! If you could only act on two or three of the things you have written down, what would they be and why?

+ Take a moment to consider your unique gifts and talents. What do you most love to do? What are you especially good at, that's unique to you? Write down your observations. With these reflections in mind, think of a current project that you are putting a lot of time and energy into. How could you tweak it to be a better fit for you? What could you de-prioritize or outsource to help you focus?

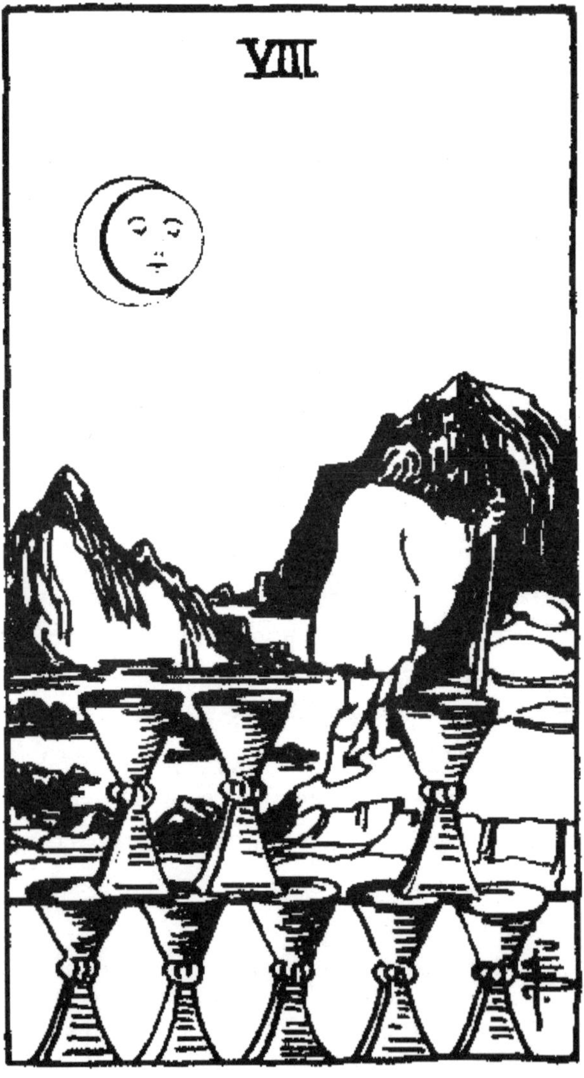
VIII

EIGHT OF CUPS

You've been a member of your church for your entire life. Your family is one of the founding families and your parents are both involved in the church's work. Many a march started from the church car park during the Civil Rights Movement.

As a young adult, you stood out for your 'Christian values' and oratory skills. Which, in your community means following a path into the ministry. The reverend has already written your recommendation letter for the Masters of Divinity programme at the same Ivy League school he attended. With your community service and high grades, you're a shoo-in.

The thing is, you've always felt like something else was out there. That there's room for more than just one deity in your life. Perhaps the all-knowing, all-seeing God you were raised with has different names and faces, all with one thing in common – love. You aren't sure where it will lead, but you are sure that an alternative spiritual path awaits you: a chance to find out what you really believe, on your own terms. You have no idea what you'll find.

You decide to take the path and see where it goes.

THE NUMINOUS TAROT GUIDE

The Eight of Cups signals a time to move on. The card often depicts somebody walking away from a set of eight cups, with a space showing that one cup is missing. This isn't a goodbye that's born of anger or resentment. It's a goodbye that opens a doorway on the search for something more meaningful to you.

Do you have the feeling that it's time to move on from a career, a relationship or even a place, but you can't exactly put your finger on why this is? Do you feel that perhaps something is missing in your life? The Eight of Cups asks you to follow your intuition as you seek to discover what this 'something' might be. This card signals that there is more out there waiting for you and that the time has come for you to seek it out. Use the energy of this card to help you start your journey in a new direction.

JOURNAL PROMPTS

+ Where does your intuition want you to go next? The intuitive voice can be hard to miss: it comes in quickly, delivers its message and then vanishes again. In the coming days, pay extra attention to any intuitive 'hits' about new ideas to research, new people to connect with and new places to visit. Make a note each time you feel like your intuition is speaking to you. At the end of the week, review what came up. Which will you follow up on first?

+ What prevents you from following your intuition? Bring to mind an area that you've felt called to explore, but have hesitated to dive in to. Now list all your reasons for not going there. Is it that you don't have time? That others will be upset with you? Whatever part of you tends to come up with these excuses, thank them for trying to protect you from any potential danger that may lie ahead and let them know you're ready to take the risk.

NINE OF CUPS

You're 'supposed' to go straight home and start making dinner, but you just don't feel like it. You've put in a long, hard day at work. It's been a good one and you've achieved a lot, but now you just need some space to decompress, without navigating the family logistics of the evening meal.

The sun is slowly setting over the city, having put in a long day itself. It's beautiful. A warm, orange glow reflects off the windows of your office building. You smile and get in the car.

The drive home is uneventful. But instead of taking your usual route to go home, you keep going until you reach the beach. There she is: the sea, waiting to tell you: 'Good job'. You park the car, get out and start walking towards the water. You even take off your shoes so you can feel the sand between your toes.

You smile at the sun as it begins to sink gradually below the horizon. 'Today was a good day, my friend,' you say. 'Let's do it again tomorrow.'

The Nine of Cups represents fulfilment: not just physically or financially, but emotionally as well. The card typically depicts a person sitting in front of a table stacked with nine cups. They wear a big smile on their face and their arms are crossed. Perhaps they seem slightly smug, but their sense of satisfaction is well earned.

After fighting and struggling to achieve your wishes and desires, the Nine of Cups signals that it's time to take a moment to enjoy a sense of accomplishment for what you have achieved. Use the energy of this card to tap into the emotional relief that comes with having met a goal, like a marathon winner breaking into sobs as they cross the finish line. The Nine of Cups can also signal the achievement of finally being comfortable with expressing emotions and enjoying the relief you experience once they're released.

JOURNAL PROMPTS

+ Take a moment to zoom out from the busy details of your day-to-day life and survey how far you have come. In your mind's eye, visit the person you were five years ago. What were their hopes, fears and aspirations? What were they working on? Now write about how these have come to fruition, in both obvious and subtle ways. What would you tell this past version of yourself about what they were struggling with then and what is to come?

+ How do you reward yourself for a job well done? Do you take a moment to give yourself a pat on the back and conduct an internal 'performance review'? Or do you tend to have your sights on your next goal before you've even accomplished the one you're working on? Plan ahead for how you will mark your next achievement, whenever and whatever that may be. Create an itinerary for how you will celebrate and revisit it when that day eventually arrives.

TEN OF CUPS

Each time you attend the annual family reunion, you know that at some point, someone is going to make a quip about either your hair, your tattoos, your job (or lack of), your living situation, your partner or any other thing they can think of to pick on. It's enough to make you not want to attend. But your grandparents are getting older and more frail. They probably won't be around for much longer.

You arrive at the house, ready for the usual onslaught of criticism. You scan the room for your judgemental relatives, almost hoping they will hurl the insults early so you can at least enjoy the meal in peace. You lock eyes with your harshest critic as they bound over to you.

But a weird thing happens next and that is… nothing. They just open their arms and hug you. 'Welcome! It's so good to see you,' they say.

You all head to the table and join the other family members. It looks like you will be able to eat in peace after all. All together as a family.

The Ten of Cups represents harmony, peace and prosperity. There's a sense of wellbeing, communal happiness and support with this card, which traditionally shows a 'family' dancing under a rainbow and ten cups. The cups form a shining, protective umbrella of nurture and support.

It can be easy to expect the worst in a situation, especially when it involves family members who may not share the same values and world view as you. But the Ten of Cups asks you to see the good in your loved ones. It encourages you to expect the best and celebrate what you do have in common: your humanity and desire for connection. When you pull this card, try to find the good surrounding you and don't just honour it – embrace it. It may be hard to see sometimes, but it's always there.

JOURNAL PROMPTS

+ Despite our differences, list the qualities that you believe we all share as human beings, even if we have different ways of expressing them. What do we all need? We may share opposing views and beliefs, but what common values lie underneath? If you are experiencing discord with anybody in your life, use this list to help you see past any turbulence on the surface to find the commonalities that lie beneath.

+ What conversation have you been putting off for fear that it will lead to conflict or hurt feelings on both sides? Now flip these fears on their heads and write a script for how the conversation might lead to a positive outcome instead. How can you frame what you have to say in a way that takes the other person's needs into account? How might they respond in a way that surprises and empowers you?

PAGE of CUPS.

PAGE OF CUPS

A cruise was certainly not your idea of a dream holiday, but the ticket was cheap and you had a week of holiday time to use up. You certainly didn't think you'd find romance on board (so clichéd!). But you do.

It's the third night of the cruise when a fellow traveller works up the nerve to approach you at the bar. They're older – as in 20 years older – and completely not your type. Which is what you love about the situation.

You chat, flirt and dance the night away. Their charm makes up for them not knowing any of the songs the DJ plays in the ship's disco. The lovemaking that night makes up for it as well. For the following three days, you are inseparable, locked in your cabin and missing all the ports of call. Then the holiday comes to an end.

The two of you exchange numbers, email addresses and social media handles. But as you return home, something tells you you'll never hear from them again.

It turns out that you're right – you don't. But ultimately, you're okay with that.

The Page of Cups brings opportunities for you to express your emotions, needs and desires freely, with no strings attached. The card suggests that if you allow yourself to be open and vulnerable, there may even be a few surprises in store – including surprises in love. The person on the card – the Page – is usually depicted holding a single cup. In some decks, the card shows a fish jumping out of the cup as the Page looks on.

This card wants you to be honest about your emotional needs. To stop guarding them so close out of fear of being hurt and let them flow. When was the last time you allowed yourself to feel or want something without judgement? The Page of Cups asks, 'How about having it now?' This card reminds us that even though opening your heart is a risk, boy, can those risks be fun.

JOURNAL PROMPTS

+ What pleasurable experiences do you tend to back out of before they've even begun? Allow your heart to take the lead, with all its childish appreciation for sheer fun, and write about an ideal day where you move from one enjoyable activity to the next. Fill in as many details as possible and notice what physical sensations arise in your body as you write. Why would you deny yourself a day like this? What is there to feel guilty about?

+ Bring to mind a time when you allowed yourself to open up and be vulnerable and it backfired. If this is a painful memory, approach it gently, slowing down your breathing and taking deep, slow belly breaths. As if you are writing to that version of yourself, write a note validating any feelings of hurt or disappointment that are present, beginning with: 'It makes sense that you feel…'. Now remind this part of yourself that these feelings are in the past and that it's safe to try again.

KNIGHT of CUPS.

KNIGHT OF CUPS

You saw a place where you and your family could live with room to grow, surrounded by nature and away from the overcrowding and pollution of the city. Your partner saw a dilapidated old shed that screamed 'money pit'. But you didn't care. They didn't have the same visionary abilities as you. This was going to be your 'forever home'.

It cost a lot less than the other houses in the area, which should have been a warning. But for you, it was an opportunity to live a dream, and that dream life was going to be perfect. And so was the house.

A year later, the roof is still leaking and you're still laboriously sanding down the hardwood floors you discovered under the linoleum; at least the floorboards weren't rotten. The new windows still haven't arrived and the house is freezing. And you haven't even started on the second floor yet. Your dream has morphed into a nightmare.

The Knight of Cups is the card of big, juicy dreams and wishes. It is the card of throwing off the shackles of inhibition and diving into love. Whatever the Knight desires, and whatever they want, they will go for it – or at least try. The card often shows a figure extending their cup as an offering. Their feelings are front and centre, leading the charge, outshining everything else. But this card can also signal illusions and flights of fancy.

The Knight of Cups asks you to go big or go home with your fantasies. The intense energy of the Knight, combined with the emotional nature of Cups, creates a swirl of magical thinking that's easy to get caught up in. This card signals a time to override logic and to act on pure emotion. But take care not to get swept away to the point where your feelings are leading you down a path of delusion.

JOURNAL PROMPTS

+ If logic were no object in your current situation, what would your heart have you do? Try to imagine you have the ability to switch off the logical left hemisphere of your brain and to allow the more intuitive right side to write an action plan for the coming weeks. What priorities emerge? What becomes less important? How does this right-brain perspective bring you closer to living your dream?

+ It can be hard to tell the difference between 'dreaming big' and 'deluding yourself' – one is the function of imagination and the other fantasy. The difference? When we're in a place of imagination, we feel inspired to take action on our visions. If we're lost in fantasy, though, our dreams tend to stay stuck in our heads. Neither is right or wrong. But when it comes to 'living the dream', what actions can you take to bring your dreams to life? Write these in your journal.

QUEEN of CUPS.

QUEEN OF CUPS

'I hate you. Get out!' Your daughter rarely loses her cool, but you've just heard her hissing at her little brother. She hasn't really been herself for the past week or so, but her mood swings are really starting to escalate now.

Your son comes down the stairs in tears. 'I only wanted to get my game back from her. She took it last week and never returned it. She screamed at me when I asked for it back,' he says

You know it's time to intervene. Her attitude is becoming unbearable. And now she's sobbing, too.

'Honey, can we talk?' you ask, speaking to her closed door.

'No. Go away. I hate all of you!' she screams from within her bedroom.

You have no idea what's going on with her, but you know she needs to talk, even if she doesn't think so just yet.

So you sit down outside her door and steel yourself for an agonizingly long wait.

The energy of the Queen of Cups can be summed up with one word: care. The Queen is usually depicted as a monarch sitting on a throne surrounded by water. She is holding a large chalice with both hands. This card signals strong, consistent, 'motherly' energy. The Queen holds space for those who need kindness, nurturing or a safe space in which they can let their emotions flow.

The Queen of Cups asks: 'Are you able to hold space for others when they need to release?' If you feel yourself wobble at the thought of this, use the Queen's energy to create space for yourself to release any pent-up emotions first. Only once that is done will you have the emotional space for others. Another way to work with this card is to contribute towards creating emotionally supportive surroundings. The Queen gives you permission to take the lead in creating a gentler, kinder space.

JOURNAL PROMPTS

+ What are some ways in which you could embody the Queen of Cups in your workplace or at home? This means considering what 'holding space' for others means for you, so begin by writing down what comes up when you think about this concept. Perhaps it means listening more, or learning to manage your own emotional reactions so you don't project them onto others. If you get stuck, consider times you have received this kind of support from other people. What made it a safe space for you?

+ Make it a priority this week to find a healthy and safe release for your own emotional backlog. Journal about a situation that has left you with some big feelings to unpack. Book a session with a therapist, healer or bodyworker whom you deeply trust. Go for a sweaty workout and imagine your pent-up feelings being worked out of your system. Or take a salt bath with some sad music playing and try to make yourself cry.

KING of CUPS.

KING OF CUPS

You're not sure who pushed whom, but things have certainly got out of hand. Lay-offs were announced last week and your team is in line to take the brunt of it. You plan to advocate for everyone to keep their jobs, but they have to be performing at their best.

And that isn't happening. Instead, all this tension has resulted in a fight.

At first, you want to send both culprits to HR, but if you do that, you know they'll be terminated immediately, which will only damage team morale even more. Perhaps you can solve the issue without getting HR involved.

That's when the idea pops into your head: invite them both to lunch at the expensive restaurant where you take your clients.

Both employees are important members of your team and you want them to feel like it. Maybe this way, you can get to the root of the problem – without anyone taking a hit.

The King of Cups is the king of compassion. He knows how and when to show it and holds himself up as an example for others to follow. The traditional imagery shows a figure sitting on a throne, holding a cup in one hand and a staff in the other. Like the Queen of the suit, the King of Cups is surrounded by water. The card represents a figure that is emotionally available, in control of their feelings and able to either give advice or take the reins of a volatile situation when needed.

This card reflects someone who is tolerant of emotional outbursts – within reason. If situations get out of hand, the King knows how to de-escalate things. Do your diplomatic skills need a tune-up? The energy of the King of Cups can be put to good use for this. This card also signals when it's time to jump in and send upset parties to their respective corners to calm down. See the King of Cups as your personal UN Secretary General.

JOURNAL PROMPTS

+ Who models King of Cups energy for you? This could be somebody from your life, or somebody in the public eye and they could be of any gender expression. List all the qualities they embody that you admire, especially when it comes to how they handle challenging situations. Now bring to mind a situation where you are being asked to display these same qualities. Are you ready to step up?

+ Think of a situation where you have played the role of the King of Cups. What was it that helped you display the level of emotional maturity required to de-escalate a volatile situation? Perhaps this meant simply walking away before things blew up, or choosing not to react to somebody trying to get a rise out of you. Remember how it felt to become this stoic version of yourself and give this 'you' a name. Call on them as needed.

ACE of PENTACLES

ACE OF PENTACLES

Applying for a small business loan can be a harrowing experience for anyone. For you, though, the thought is enough to make you physically ill. But you've always wanted to be your own boss and you think the neighbourhood could use some new businesses to inject much-needed funds into the community.

First you need to find the money. You come across a company specializing in small business loans and fill in the introductory survey.

The big day comes and it's time to go over rates and fees face-to-face.

The small talk with the loan officer is polite, but when you pull out your presentation and explain your idea, they fall completely silent.

'Have I screwed up?' you ask yourself.

Actually, no. Your idea is brilliant. *You* are brilliant. And you get the loan.

Now get to work and make it happen.

The Ace of Pentacles signifies a shift from the planning, dreaming and talking stage of an idea to taking concrete action. It shows that an opportunity is right in front of you, so close that you could almost touch it, if you'd just stretch yourself a little.

The suit of Pentacles focuses our attention on the tangible things in our lives: work, home, money, our bodies. The Ace of Pentacles opens the door towards acquiring or working with them in some way. The card usually shows a hand appearing from a cloud, offering a coin.

Do you talk a good game? Great. But can you follow this up with action? If you're having difficulties putting your money where your mouth is so you can get started, the energy of this Ace can give you a loving push. Meditate on the Ace of Pentacles to start doing what you need to do to get what you want to get. The energy of the Ace prepares you to work – and work hard – to reach your goal.

JOURNAL PROMPTS

+ What common fears tend to stall you when it comes to acting on your ideas? With your current situation in mind, list all the things that come up when you consider moving forwards in some way. What 'buts' and 'what ifs' are standing in your way? Now think back to a past situation when stalling meant you missed out on an opportunity. Were some of the same fears present then? Which fears are valid and which are holding you back?

+ Consider all the resources you will need to have in place to move an idea from the dreaming stage to actually making it happen. Do you need financial investment? Time in your schedule? Assistance from others? List everything you can think of and, for each thing you note down, add a line about how you can begin to put these pieces together. What will be your next step?

TWO OF PENTACLES

You're the only person of colour where you work. Even though office camaraderie has been good, you still feel the need to prove you belong here. You were hired during the company's diversity push, which was well meaning, but left you politically vulnerable.

You juggle multiple responsibilities to prove you're as good as your CV says. You also want to make sure that when the next leadership programme opens up, you'll be in the running for a spot.

After a year of working yourself to the bone and taking on every assignment handed to you, you're ready to talk with your boss about the programme.

Yes, you've done well. And the fact that you've done so well in accomplishing all of your goals has signalled to your boss that you are ready.

Not ready for the leadership programme, according to her, but ready for even more tasks.

The Two of Pentacles is the card of multitasking. It often shows a person juggling two coins in their hands while balancing on one foot. It signals the ability to be flexible and handle multiple challenges and is also a gentle reminder to have fun with these challenges, if possible. It can also reflect a need to balance issues such as finances or career.

Use this card's energy to examine how agile you are and whether that agility is helping or hurting your wellbeing. On the one hand, 'the hustle' can be invigorating. It means things are happening and moving forwards. When this is the case, the effort put into your work is enjoyable.

On the other hand, hustling can wear you out. What is the psychological toll? How are you handling the pressures of work, family, money and so on? Is it at least enjoyable? Are you getting anything out of it? The Two of Pentacles can prompt you to answer these questions.

JOURNAL PROMPTS

+ Create a pie chart of life, with a 'slice' for each of the following areas: work, relationships, wellbeing, family, creativity and spirituality. Determine the size of each 'slice' based on the amount of time and energy you are currently dedicating to each of these elements. Where is there an imbalance? How might your energy levels and sense of life satisfaction improve if you spread yourself more evenly?

+ Is there an area in your life where you feel you are being taken advantage of? Where you are putting in the work (this could be physical, mental or emotional labour) and not getting what you need in return? Whatever comes to mind, journal about how this makes you feel. How can you take steps to ensure that you're getting out what you put in?

THREE OF PENTACLES

You've been watching the news and know bad weather is on the way. There isn't much time and you needed to board up the house before evacuating to the school gym. But in the rush to get your stuff loaded into the car, you sprain your wrist.

'No worries,' you say to yourself. 'I can still get everything boarded up and get myself out of here.'

The problem is that you can't. Not with that wrist. But damn it, asking for help isn't in your vocabulary.

The Taylors watch you from their porch and shake their 80-year-old heads. 'That child's going to get herself killed,' Mr Taylor says. The couple have no plans to leave themselves, but are keeping a watchful eye on you.

You feel a tap on your shoulder. It's Mrs Taylor. 'Let us help,' she says.

You accept. After everything is secured, you look at the old couple's home. 'Now let's secure your place,' you say to them. 'Then you're coming with me.'

The Three of Pentacles represents planning, support and organization. It's the card of confidence and trusting that you and those around you have the skills needed to do the job. The RWS deck shows three people on the card: a stonemason standing on a bench, with tools in hand, in conference with two colleagues standing below. Three pentacles are embedded into the stonework arch over their heads.

Are you feeling scattered about a task? Perhaps a tad overwhelmed and not sure which path to take? Use the energy of the Three of Pentacles to help you strategize about how to get things done. And if you can't do it all yourself, ask for help. This card celebrates the coordination of goals and a combining of efforts. The Three of Pentacles reflects the advantages of good preparation and thinking ahead.

JOURNAL PROMPTS

+ Make three lists: one of things you do exceptionally well, one of things you can get done if needed and one of things that are most definitely not in your wheelhouse. Why are you spending any time attempting to tackle anything on the last list? Or the second list, for that matter? With this in mind, look at your current situation and think about what you can outsource and to whom. What would be the knock-on effect on your energy levels and wellbeing?

+ When was the last time you asked for help and how did it feel? What about the last time you were able to help somebody else? Our society praises independence and many modern conveniences are designed to make us less reliant on others. But what is lost when we value independence over interdependence? Journal about what comes up.

FOUR OF PENTACLES

The house has been in your family for at least a century. But it has now become a burden. The older family members died years ago and only you and your cousin are left. It makes no sense to keep it, but your cousin refuses to sell, becoming enraged and offended whenever you bring the topic up.

'How about you just buy me out?' you suggest, during a tense conversation. 'Then you can do whatever you want.'

'How dare you! You seem to have forgotten the sacrifices our great-grandparents made to buy this land and build the house! You're a disgrace to the family!' your cousin replies.

Their words make absolutely no sense. You know there has to be something more to this. It isn't only about the house.

'Cousin, tell me. What do you think you'll lose if we sell?'

You hear them exhale. Then, with their voice cracking, they say, 'I'm afraid I'll lose you. That property is the only thing that connects us.'

Now it all makes sense.

'No. What connects us is... us. And selling the property won't change that.'

The Four of Pentacles often shows a figure tightly gripping one pentacle. Three more pentacles surround them. There's a strong feeling of possession associated with the Four of Pentacles, which represents trying to keep hold of what's yours – or what you think is yours. This could either stem from a desire to retain possession of something you've rightfully earned, or from a fear of something being taken away. The common denominator in both cases is control.

When you pull this card, you're being asked to look at what you are so determined to hold on to. What are you unwilling to put down or let go? Is holding on worth the effort, or is it time to loosen your grip? The Four of Pentacles also signals a tendency to be greedy – or at least miserly – when, perhaps, there's no real need. This card wants you to examine what it's worth letting go of, not in the name of losing something, but in the name of making space for something more.

JOURNAL PROMPTS

+ What are you clinging on to without even realizing it? This could be a physical thing (or things) that you are hoarding; a relationship with somebody you can't imagine not having in your life; or a belief system that has come to define the way you see the world. Just for a moment, imagine letting this thing go. Notice all the feelings this brings up. Beyond any immediate sense of loss, what else is present for you?

+ What is your relationship to control? It's human nature to seek to control the world around us, which we often do by creating 'stories' in our heads to help explain why things are the way they are. But when we get too attached to these stories ('X means Y is always going to happen', or 'things are this way because of Z'), we inadvertently close the door on infinite potential possibilities for change. What stories are you telling yourself with regards to your current situation?

FIVE OF PENTACLES

Your bank balance is in the negative again and the overdraft charges and penalties are just making things worse.

Your utilities, including your phone, are about to be disconnected due to missed payments. Your phone is your only form of communication with work. It's how you find out how many shifts you're scheduled for at the shop. It's how you know what days you're working. It's your life.

You're about to panic.

Stop. Think for a second.

What's the quickest way for you to stem the financial haemorrhaging? How can you get back at least a little bit of control over your financial situation?

You don't like the answer, but it's the only one you can come up with. First, you'll close the bank account. It'll affect your credit rating, but that's already in a nosedive. Second, you'll call your phone provider and set up a payment plan to get back on track.

It's not the best solution, but it's the only one available to you right now.

The Five of Pentacles usually represents a loss in the material world, for example in finances, health or career. The RWS deck shows two figures – one on crutches and the other wrapped in threadbare clothing – walking past a window featuring five pentacles. It's cold and snowing: a sad, miserable scene.

The Five of Pentacles signals setbacks and overall despair. It focuses mostly on the material world, but can also reflect a sense of feeling excluded.

It's a card that reflects doubts and the sense that things are so bad, there's no way out. Are you facing financial troubles? Do you feel as if everyone is getting ahead in their career except for you? The Five of Pentacles acknowledges your worries, but suggests that they're only temporary. Its medicine for you is to remind you that the only way to get out of a challenging situation is to keep your wits about you and to keep walking through it.

JOURNAL PROMPTS

+ Whether or not you are facing financial or other material world challenges right now, think of a time from your past when you've been in a situation like this and use it to come up with a positive affirmation to help you when the going gets tough. Write down a list of all the inner and outer resources you were able to draw on then. When you're finished, review the list and come up with an 'I am' statement that lets you know you're going to be okay.

+ Who can you ask for help and who can you offer help to? When faced with the kinds of challenges shown by this card, it can feel like the weight of the world is on your shoulders and it's easy forget that assistance is all around you. Remind yourself of this by making a list of all the people you can reach out to when times are hard. In addition, think about who *you* can help out today. Being of service to others is another potent reminder that we are built for interdependence and that it feels good to help others in need.

SIX OF PENTACLES

She's one of your closest friends and always has money to burn. She married very well and has a tendency to drop little reminders about that fact whenever you're together.

She's always the one to pick up the bill and you dine out together at the best restaurants in town. When she invites you on one of her legendary shopping trips, you usually come home with a new addition to your wardrobe.

You love her, with or without her money. But things get tricky when she's lonely or depressed.

Or drunk.

She calls you in the middle of the day while you're at work and gets angry when you don't answer. She texts you at night while you're asleep and wonders why you don't respond immediately.

It makes you wonder sometimes: does she buy you things because she loves you? Or because she needs you?

THE NUMINOUS TAROT GUIDE

The Six of Pentacles reflects the haves, the have nots and the balance of power between these two groups. The card often shows two people in need kneeling on the ground, with their hands raised to accept coins coming from above them. Whether the message of the Six of Pentacles is positive or negative will depend upon the context: it can represent power plays and domination, or it can represent giving and receiving and the ability to accept offers of help.

Meditate on the Six of Pentacles to closely examine the relationships in your life and the material balances of power that define them. Is someone using money and power to exert their dominance over you? Are you perhaps doing this to someone yourself? What actions could either or both of you take in order to correct this? The Six of Pentacles also asks you to look at the 'why' behind any imbalance. Are you allowing it to continue by not standing up for yourself? This card can help you even the score.

JOURNAL PROMPTS

+ How good are you at sharing? The desire to accumulate material wealth (in terms of money, food, shelter and other resources) stems from a desire for security. But what about when we have more that we 'need'? Fear that what we've acquired can be taken away may lead to greed. This also signals a lack of trust in our ability to repeat what we've done to acquire these things. In the coming days, practise building this particular trust muscle by giving something away each day. Notice what comes back to you in return.

+ What charitable cause tugs at your heart strings? Do some research about organizations that are doing good in this area and commit to making a monthly donation – whatever you can afford. Each month, when the money leaves your bank account, visualize it helping a person or group of people in need. When you picture this now, journal about how this makes you feel.

SEVEN OF PENTACLES

A new salon has opened up around the corner and you like the braider's work. Each style is intricate and artistic. You only want individual braids, which shouldn't be that difficult, right?

One appointment and hours later, you're still in the styling chair. The braider has misjudged the thickness of your hair.

Your anger grows with each passing minute. The braider tries her best to speed up, but your patience has worn thin. 'How in the world can you call yourself a professional braider and still be taking this long?' you sneer.

You can see she is considering a response, carefully weighing her words as she finishes an extension. She stands and turns your chair around so you can see yourself in the mirror. You can't believe the beauty you see. The braider is doing an exquisite job. The braids that are slowly appearing on your crown aren't just a style: they're a work of art.

'I have a suggestion,' you say, as you smile. 'How about we both take a 15-minute break to stretch our legs? Then I'll let you get back to work.'

The Seven of Pentacles represents taking a step back and taking stock. It often shows a person pausing in the middle of what seems like hard, back-breaking work. Seven pentacles sit before them as they analyse the results of their efforts. The temptation might be to give up at this point – but remember, all that's needed is a breather.

Are you so deep into a task or project that you can't see the proverbial wood for the trees? Pulling this card can suggest that you're lacking perspective and that your goal has become obscured with analysis, doubts and distractions. The Seven of Pentacles asks you to take a few steps back. Not only will you be able to see how far you have to go, you'll also be reminded of how much you've already achieved.

JOURNAL PROMPTS

+ Wherever you're at with a current project, it's time for a time-out. If this doesn't seem possible, take a moment to map out how to achieve what you need to. Maybe you can ask for an extension on a deadline? If you were to take a physical break, where could you go and what activities would help completely take your mind off the task at hand? Jot down any ideas that come up. How do you think your project would benefit from creating this space to refresh your thinking?

+ Think about your relationship with the concept of 'rest'. Write down all the things that come up for you when you consider what kinds of people 'deserve' to take a break, and under what circumstances. Is rest something that must be earned? Is it as valuable a part of the creation process as the end result? Review what you have written down. Where did these beliefs come from? Are they true for you?

EIGHT OF PENTACLES

Everyone thought you were crazy when you decided to go back to college to get your bachelor's degree. You had a good life and a wonderful family, complete with kids and grandkids.

There was nothing left to prove – except to yourself.

You applied to the local college, with nothing but a high school education from the 1980s and 'life experience' to put on your application. And you got in.

It was four years of absolute hell, which included balancing your classes and home life, studying long hours and relearning how to actually *learn* – a woefully underrated skill.

But you kept at it. And today you stand with your classmates, one of whom is your granddaughter, and prepare to walk across the stage to accept your degree.

Yes, you had a good life. And now it's even better.

The Eight of Pentacles signals perseverance, dedication and sticking to a monotonous, arduous task in order to reach a goal. The card often shows a person working hard, hammering away at a pentacle. A finished pentacle is on the ground; six more hang above them. The energy of the Eight of Pentacles is one of plain ol' grafting.

Keeping your eye on a long-term goal can be difficult, especially when you're in the thick of the ongoing labour of bringing it to fruition. But the hard work *will* pay off. The message of this card is simple: keep going. When the Eight of Pentacles shows up, it's a reminder that you may get tired – you may even get discouraged. But it's also a reminder that these are only waypoints and perfectly normal states of being when your nose is to the grindstone. So don't give up.

JOURNAL PROMPTS

+ Bring to mind a time when you completed a project that seemed to go on forever. Looking back at this situation, how did you summon the strength and perseverance to keep going during the moments when it felt like you would never reach your goal? Note down anything that comes up. Now use these observations to come up with a personal mantra for when you find yourself in a similar situation. What can you remind yourself of to help you keep going?

+ Often when we have a goal in our sights we fixate on the end result, while diminishing the importance of the daily work required to bring it to fruition. How can you bring more value to this part of the process, instead of focusing all your energy on the outcome? It's the small, everyday actions that make up the overall texture of our lives. Today, and in the coming days, take a moment to acknowledge and even celebrate each miniscule 'win'.

NINE OF PENTACLES

You've pulled a double shift and you're exhausted.

The hospital has been at full capacity all day and you and your fellow nurses have been pushed to the absolute limit: a multi-car pile-up with serious injuries; police officers who refused to respect the fact that suspects deserve medical treatment, no matter what they're accused of; and doctors who questioned each and every decision you made.

It's time to go home.

Instead of cooking tonight, you stop at a restaurant and pick up a takeaway. Next up, you make a quick dash into a department store for your favourite jasmine-scented bath oil. As you're walking out, you notice a sale on pyjamas. A luxury compared to the T-shirt and sweatpants you normally wear to bed. You choose a set and add them to your basket, too.

When you get home, you recount the day, reflect on how hard you've worked and remember that there will be more of the same tomorrow.

But right now, your thoughts turn to the bath. And the new pyjamas that await you.

The Nine of Pentacles is the card of grace and leisure and of taking a moment to feel proud of yourself without smugness. The card often features a person walking through a lush garden with nine pentacles at their feet. Perched on their hand is a falcon, representing graceful control. The Nine of Pentacles suggests an air of confidence in one's abilities, without the need to brag or receive applause or praise from others.

As such, this card gives you permission to take a break and reward yourself for a job well done. When you pull the Nine of Pentacles, take a moment to review when you last did something nice for yourself because you believed you deserved it. Do you struggle with this concept? The Nine of Pentacles is a reminder to reward yourself for your efforts.

JOURNAL PROMPTS

+ How do you reward yourself? List all the different ways that you could show yourself some appreciation in the coming days, whether this is for a job well done, for reaching a personal goal, or simply for showing up for others in a way that reflects the person you aspire to be. If you don't feel you 'deserve' a reward, ask yourself why this is. What are you failing to notice about your achievements? In what area could you challenge yourself to step up?

+ What matters more to you: personal satisfaction in a job well done, or praise and validation from others? Bring to mind a time when you have received external accolades for your work or achievements. Write about how this made you feel. Now consider a time when you were able to take quiet pride in something others may not have even noticed. Write down how this made you feel. Do these reflections alter your response to the original question?

TEN OF PENTACLES

After working hard for over 40 years, it's finally time for you to retire. You're not exactly sure how you feel about it at the moment; not because of fear or nostalgia, but because you're still so busy.

You and your partner have met with the advisors at your bank and with the pension fund to discuss your plans to make sure they're financially sound. The only thing left is to tell the rest of your family what you're planning: you're going to sell the house. It's too big and too expensive to take care of at your age anyway. You and your partner will take part of the money to pay for a small, hip apartment in the happening part of town – not too far from where you grew up.

The rest of the money from the house will go to your kids, which they can use to build their own financial security. They won't have to wait until you leave this earth. They'll get to enjoy the fruits of your labour now, alongside you.

The Ten of Pentacles represents abundance and material security. The card usually depicts an older person sitting and observing a couple with a child walking near them. Ten pentacles dominate the foreground. As such, this card signals family prosperity and any kind of inheritance that is passed down through the generations. Wealth and good fortune are being shared with those who come after.

Regardless of your financial situation, use the energy of the Ten of Pentacles to help you focus on creating stability for yourself and your loved ones by making solid decisions that move you in the direction of material stability. The card also asks you to look at your family and ancestral traditions, to see which can be integrated into your life today. If that's not feasible, consider creating your own traditions to pass on to those who are to come after you.

JOURNAL PROMPTS

+ What are all the things you have inherited, and stand to inherit, from your family of origin? As well as any material hand-me-downs and heirlooms, consider the traditions and beliefs that are bestowed on members of your clan. These may or may not be positive, or things that reflect you as an individual, but they are part of your heritage nonetheless. Journal on how you can work with the vestiges of your lineage to create more abundance for yourself and others.

+ What will your legacy be? Consider where you are focusing your energy in your life today. What might be the longer-term implications of your current actions – both for your immediate family members and for those making up our wider family? Now consider what you would like to leave behind. Note down anything that comes up. How can you adjust your goals to begin putting things in place?

PAGE of PENTACLES.

PAGE OF PENTACLES

Saving has never been your strong point. Cash has always flowed through your hands like water, often leaving you with too much 'month' at the end of your money. After years of budgeting fiascos, you wish you could get the hang of this cash-flow thing, but you are still slightly offended when a friend suggests you attend a money management course. You decide to go along anyway – you've got nothing to lose.

Boy, are you glad you did. You've always thought one had to *have* money in order to save it. But you knuckle down and learn about micro-savings techniques and all the small things you can do to cut your monthly costs, such as not eating out every day for lunch, or calling your insurance company to enquire about discounts for good drivers.

After using your newly acquired budgeting skills for six months, not only are you able to start a savings account, but you can also pay back the money you've owed your friend since last year.

Which is probably why they recommended the course in the first place.

The Page of Pentacles brings a message of practical study: of being so intent on mastering something that you're willing to focus all your attention on it, be it a new skill, an opportunity or a physical thing. The card often depicts a young person holding a pentacle in their hand, gazing upon it as if they're sizing it up. This card signals a desire to learn and to use what you discover to achieve results.

The Page of this suit wants you to trust and encourage yourself to put in the work needed to succeed in what you desire. It suggests being willing to start afresh, with a beginner's mind, to gain a 360-degree understanding of what you're trying to accomplish. Are you ready to learn a new skill? Or perhaps a new way of managing a situation? The energy of the Page of Pentacles can help you open your mind and go back to the drawing board in order to get what you need.

JOURNAL PROMPTS

+ What is something you've always been curious about learning how to do, but have never had the time, energy, finances or drive to commit to? Perhaps it's a specific skill, or maybe it's just a subject you've always been fascinated by. Whatever it is, take a moment in the coming days to do some research online about what courses, webinars, books and mentorship is available in this area. There's something there for you.

+ In what area of life could you benefit from adopting a 'beginner's' mindset? A clue to this would be an area where you are certain that you 'know it all' and could never be convinced to think or act differently. What is it that makes you so sure about *your* way of doing this thing? Write out all the beliefs that are attached to it, then review your list and challenge yourself to see it from a different perspective. What possibilities open up?

KNIGHT of PENTACLES.

KNIGHT OF PENTACLES

Your 75-year-old grandfather is proud to tell anyone within earshot that he always bought his groceries on sale, only showered using cold water and owns only one good suit, which he's worn since the day your mother was born.

But now you're getting married. And you'd like your grandfather to walk you down the aisle – ideally wearing something other than a shiny polyester suit from the 1970s.

'Grandad, please. I'm begging you. It's a black-tie wedding. Your suit is lemon yellow,' you say, as you hold back tears of frustration.

'What's wrong with that?' he asks. 'It was fashionable back in the day.'

'Yes. But that was then. Come on. You've worked hard all your life. Don't you think you deserve to splurge on yourself just once?' you ask.

'You just don't want me to embarrass you,' he says.

You know he's right.

The Knight of Pentacles presents a conundrum. The card shows a knight holding a pentacle as they sit on a horse. They're not moving; they remain fixed in place. There's a feeling of stagnation and stodginess with this card; an attitude of 'all work and no play'. It's a card of caution veering towards inflexibility – but, like the Eight of the suit, it can also represent discipline and sticking with a situation until the end.

The Knight of Pentacles asks if you're being too hesitant about taking a chance. After all, with risk comes opportunity. When this card appears, it may be a warning that your rigidity means you're about to let a new opening pass you by. On the other hand, depending on the context, the Knight can be a signal for you to slow your roll. Check your budget and your stamina. If either or both are lacking, the energy of this card can help you stop to replenish your reserves.

JOURNAL PROMPTS

+ Bring to mind one thing about your current situation that feels like a 'sticking point' for you. Now try to determine whether this is because you *can't* move forwards (maybe you don't have all the support or resources you need) don't *want* to (perhaps you have become too comfortable where you are), or that it's just too soon to move on (perhaps you feel you still have more to learn right here). With clarity on this, what should the next move be?

+ Our society is obsessed with progress and forwards motion, but it's unwise to keep moving forwards without acknowledging and integrating past learning and experiences. If you're finding it hard to make progress, consider what elements from your past you have not quite integrated yet. Journal about what comes to mind.

QUEEN of PENTACLES

QUEEN OF PENTACLES

You've just made it home and want to rest when your 13-year-old daughter walks through the door with tears in her eyes. When you ask her what's wrong, she says she doesn't want to talk about it.

During dinner, she is almost silent, only making polite conversation to head off any more questions. You finally push your plate to the side and force eye contact with her.

'Honey, what's wrong?' you ask again.

After about half a minute, she finally tells you. 'There's nothing wrong with me mom. It's Paulina.'

Paulina is her best friend.

'What's going on with Paulina?' you ask.

'She came out to her folks. And they kicked her out.'

You're stunned. Not at Paulina's coming out, but her parents' response. 'Where is she now?' you ask.

'Hanging out at the library. She has nowhere to go. They kicked her out two days ago.'

You get up and grab your keys. 'Come on. We're going to get her.'

The Queen of Pentacles reflects a physically nurturing energy. The card typically shows the Queen sitting on a throne with a pentacle in her hands, with a lush nature scene in the background. The Queen uses the feminine energy of caring and nurturing to provide comfort and sustenance where required. She makes sure that everybody has whatever they might need.

The Queen of Pentacles provides maternal stability to those around her and is the calm in the eye of the storm; the soothing comfort that consoles a child after they've woken up from a nightmare. Allow this card to ground you and to help you find your centre when you're nervous. The Queen is also warm and practical. The energy of this card can help you examine exactly why you're afraid and what concrete steps you can take to address this fear.

JOURNAL PROMPTS

+ Think about an individual – or individuals – who embody Queen of Pentacles energy for you. This could be somebody you know, or somebody in the public eye. What qualities do they exhibit that reflect the energy of this card? Write them down. Now bring to mind a time when you have felt nervous and unsure (perhaps you are feeling this way now). What would this person say to help soothe, comfort and inspire you?

+ What material sustenance or self-care can you offer yourself that will help you feel more nurtured and held? Perhaps it's a favourite meal, some form of physical pampering or some cosy time curled up with a book. Maybe a particular person comes to mind and it's time for you to reach out and give them a call. Whatever it is, make some space in your schedule to give yourself what your soul needs in the coming days.

KING of PENTACLES.

KING OF PENTACLES

You've been in the music business long enough to know how it works. And you know that these three beautiful, talented female vocalists in their final year of high school will make any record company a lot of money.

When you first listened to their demo, you knew they were special. But you want to talk to them first.

You meet them for lunch at a burger place near their school. The young women are sweet, smart and extremely talented. One wants to be a doctor, another wants to become an architect. The last one hopes to go to art school.

They can all sing, too, and all three have star potential. But fame is fleeting. You know this – you started out as a singer yourself. After talking to them for what seems like hours, and getting along well, you make a suggestion.

'How about you three go to college? At least for a year. If you like it there, stay. If you really think you want to become professional singers, here's my number. But I want all of you to try getting an education first.'

The King of Pentacles represents dependability and having the wisdom to see all facets of an opportunity. The card often shows the King sitting on his throne with a pentacle in one hand. The card often signals reliability, competence and generosity.

The King has the aura of somebody who assumes responsibility without a second thought and provides a solid foundation and support. They think before they speak and, when they do, they offer sound, dependable guidance. The King of Pentacles is sensible and committed to his goals. When this card appears, it's asking for good, solid thinking. Are you up for the challenge? Can you provide grounded leadership and build trust? Use the energy of this King to establish a solid foundation for yourself and those around you.

JOURNAL PROMPTS

+ What actions and behaviours create an environment of trust? Focusing on times and spaces where you have felt safe and like you could rely on the people involved, write down all the things that come to mind about what helped to create this sense of safety and dependability. When you're done, review your list and consider how you could embody more of the traits you've identified, so that you can be that person for others.

+ Do you need some King of Pentacles wisdom and advice? Whatever you are currently dealing with in your life, see if you can identify a part of you that feels unsure, bewildered or even afraid. What does this part of you need to know or hear in order feel more settled and secure? Perhaps this is something you can give voice to or model for yourself. If not, who do you think you could call on to give you the stabilizing counsel that you need?

CONCLUSION

The aim of this book has been to take what was once seen as a mysterious and perhaps slightly complicated method of divination and show how it can be applied to modern life. We hope that the stories have reminded you of your own life experiences, allowing you to link them to each card so you can use them to honour how far you've come and feel excited about how far you can go.

The tarot is 78 pieces of cardstock. But what's on that cardstock – the scenes, colours and numbers – can transport you to a place where you'll find the answers you need.

It's all in your hands.

ABOUT THE AUTHOR

Rashunda Tramble is a writer and tarot reader based in Zurich, Switzerland. Originally from Memphis, Tennessee, Tramble has worked in radio and television in the US, and marketing and communications (art, luxury and finance) in Europe. She is also a member of Mensa, the high IQ society.

Photo credit: Caroline Minjolle

ABOUT THE NUMINOUS

The Numinous is a Now Age publishing platform from Ruby Warrington, a British writer, author and thought-leader currently located in New York City. Find us @the_numinous and at www.the-numinous.com